THE CRAFT OF UNIVERSITY TEACHING

What does university teaching – as a craft – look like? What changes to a professor's educational philosophy does it require? What would a shift to a craft perspective to teaching suggest for higher education? Peter Lindsay addresses these questions in both a general sense and with respect to the everyday tasks of university professors, from the use and misuse of technology and the assignment of course readings, to the handling of academic dishonesty and the instilling of enthusiasm for learning.

Intended for professors of all academic disciplines who either enjoy teaching or wish to enjoy it more, *The Craft of University Teaching* is a provocative and accessible book containing practical advice gleaned from the academic literature on pedagogy.

In an era of increased bureaucratic oversight, rapidly diminishing budgets, and waves of technological distraction, *The Craft of University Teaching* provokes reflection on matters of pedagogy that are too often taken as settled. In so doing, it seeks to reclaim teaching as the intellectually vibrant and intrinsically rewarding endeavor that it is.

PETER LINDSAY is a professor of political science and philosophy at Georgia State University and the former director of Georgia State's Center for Teaching and Learning.

The CRAFT *of* UNIVERSITY TEACHING

✦ Peter Lindsay ✦

UNIVERSITY OF TORONTO PRESS
Toronto Buffalo London

Reprinted in paperback 2019

ISBN 978-1-4875-0323-9 (cloth)   ISBN 978-1-4875-2514-9 (paper)

♾ Printed on acid-free, 100% post-consumer recycled paper.

Library and Archives Canada Cataloguing in Publication

Title: The craft of university teaching / Peter Lindsay.

Names: Lindsay, Peter, 1958–, author.

Description: Published in hardcover in 2018. |
Includes bibliographical references and index.

Identifiers: Canadiana 2019014386X | ISBN 9781487525149 (softcover)

Subjects: LCSH: College teaching.

Classification: LCC LB2331 .L56 2019 | DDC 378.1/25 – dc23

University of Toronto Press acknowledges the financial assistance to its publishing
program of the Canada Council for the Arts and the Ontario Arts Council, an
agency of the Government of Ontario.

 **Canada Council Conseil des Arts
for the Arts du Canada**

 **ONTARIO ARTS COUNCIL
CONSEIL DES ARTS DE L'ONTARIO**
an Ontario government agency
un organisme du gouvernement de l'Ontario

 Funded by the   Financé par le   **Canadä**
Government   gouvernement
of Canada   du Canada

For Kate

Contents

Preface

Who Are You?

This question is the one I asked as I began to write this book. To whom am I writing? The answer, I came to see, is: "someone like me" – someone who is teaching in higher education and yet who thinks of herself[1] as a biologist, art historian, sociologist, or perhaps an expert on law, finance, or neurology. Someone, in other words, who spends the majority of her career teaching, but who miraculously still does not say "teacher" when asked, "what do you do?"

Such a self-conception is delusional, of course. One need not be a doctrinaire Marxist to accept that whatever clever self-images we embrace, we are what we do. A similar deceit is often seen in waiters who introduce themselves as writers even though their work and sleep schedule precludes the pen from so much as touching paper. Perhaps one day they *will be* writers, but it is difficult to see how endless repetitions of "Hello, my name is Mike, and I'll be serving you tonight" could not go to the core of one's self – which is not to suggest there is anything wrong with that self, only that it is not the self it thinks it is. Professors do not have the same daily affirmation to contend with, but after countless hours answering student emails, grading papers, and preparing classes, it takes no less wilfulness to maintain that one is more of a biologist or sociologist than a *teacher* of biology or sociology. At least the waiter/aspiring writer faces only a (perhaps) mythical future; many professors live in a mythical present.

None of this is meant to imply that professors don't do research (although most do not) or that teaching is a rung below research on the ladder of academic virtues (although it is certainly perceived that way within the culture – hence the self-deception). My point is simply that teaching is both what we do and what we often pretend not to do. And, for at least two reasons, it need not be this way.[2]

First, academics have made too much of the distinction between scholarly disciplines and the teaching of those disciplines. In producing knowledge, we are learning it. When we present it to our colleagues, we are teaching it. The manner in which a researcher knows and discovers something and the process whereby others come to grasp it are only temporally distinct. Teaching done at its best emulates the modes of inquiry employed by those who created the knowledge, and in so doing captures the intellectual excitement that accompanied that creation. The real task of teaching, in fact, is to demonstrate that the joy of learning can excite and seduce every bit as much as can the joy of research because, at the end of the day, there is no logical, conceptual, or analytic difference between the two. Once we grasp that fact, distinctions between an astronomer and a *teacher* of astronomy dissolve, taking with them our reasons for regarding the latter with any less enthusiasm than the former.

The second and more direct reason we should not deny our teaching selves gets at the reason I wrote this book. After more than thirty years of teaching, I find myself still drawn to, and fascinated by, questions in my field of study (political philosophy), and I still enjoy the research I do in that field. That said, I have also, especially over that past ten years, found myself equally drawn to, and fascinated by, questions that touch upon the experiences of being an educator – experiences that do not necessarily speak to any academic discipline in particular, but that are nonetheless intrinsically interesting and certainly worthy of scholarly reflection. What I find difficult to believe is that professors of *any* field would not feel similarly. We are for the most part inquisitive people – try completing a PhD without a sense of intellectual curiosity – so how is it possible that any among us would not wish to reflect on the activity that consumes most of our professional lives?

My hope, then, is to convince professors of chemistry, literature, history, and law that pedagogical matters are good to know not just because they help get us through the teaching day, but also for the same reason that it is good to know the structure of DNA, the intricacies of Dante, the causes of the French Revolution, the benefits of habeas corpus, or, for that matter, *any* body of knowledge to which it is worth devoting a life. If you need such convincing, because your heart lies in your research or, if you no longer do research, because your *identity* still lies with your discipline – or if, like me, you just need the occasional reminding – then it is to *you* that I address all that follows.

So what is it that follows? I would call it an interrogation of pedagogy, one conducted under the lens of craftwork. What does teaching in higher education – *as a craft* – look like? How does the manner in which we approach teaching change when it is treated as a craft? These are my core questions.

A word of warning, though: the answers to these questions might not be immediately apparent. I say this in light of another characteristic that teaching and research (at least, *good* teaching and *good* research) share – namely, the priority of the process over the outcome: the trip over the place you're going. Certainly it's good, for all one's efforts, to have learned or discovered something: to arrive. But, especially in the case of learning something, how we get there is a matter of no small importance, for it speaks to how we hold the knowledge we've acquired, which, in turn – to speak to practicalities – dictates how long we hold it. Some educational journeys are very short; we learn simply by being told: "Here are the findings." Then there are

longer journeys, those that begin: "This was the road to those findings; let's spend time on it." If your interest in a book on pedagogy is
in the short road, then there are myriad resources for you, and I cite
many of the better ones. The book in your hands, however, might not
be for you.

The model I have in mind here is less didactic than one that proposes
to "teach by telling."[3] Although I have my own set of findings – lessons
that guide *my* teaching – I shudder to think of their effects in anyone
else's hands. My interest is more modest: I'd rather point down a road
on which the questions raised, the very tentative and sometimes con-
tradictory answers proposed, and the situations depicted all find some
unique meaning in the particular educational world that you, the reader,
inhabit. Such roads are not linear. Their purpose is not to arrive at a particular end, but to provoke and prod at every turn and, in so doing, to
suggest that, however one travels and in whatever direction, it is always
best to slow down.

Don't be surprised, then, if the "findings" I offer seem more cave-
ated than categorical. And don't worry if the topics discussed seem
randomly chosen – they are, after all, just excuses to get at more fundamental pedagogical matters. And most important, don't be put off by
arguments that seem out and out flawed. In truth, every time I reread
what I wrote, I found things to disagree with. Initially this was the
source of some frustration: how could I ever finish? Over time, however, I came to see this disagreement with my own earlier ideas as a sign
that perhaps I *had* finished, or at least that I had accomplished what I
set out to accomplish. A good book should not tell its readers how to
think – far better to arouse in them the desire to reject its claims.
That the claims in this book are periodically rejected even by the
person who wrote them seems especially promising. Of course, I
might just as periodically come back to them, but when I do it is
only because those claims, right or wrong, will have spurred the
sort of reflective curiosity that lies at the heart of learning. Hence if
this book proves of value to you – if you *learn* anything from it – it

will be because whatever "findings" you glean from it will be yours, not mine.

As a terminological note, I use the word "university" – as in the title of the book – to refer to *all* institutions of higher education. American liberal arts professors, as well as professors in teaching and community colleges, are emphatically part of my target audience. I avoid "college" only because in Canada the word can also refer to institutions of secondary education. (Not that I would discourage instructors outside of higher education from reading the book. Results may vary, though.)

Acknowledgments

I should begin by acknowledging all the people whom I'm about to forget to acknowledge. This book percolated for quite a while, during which time countless colleagues, students, friends, and relatives intentionally or unintentionally contributed to its completion in some way. The problem now is that I have no way of recalling each and every one of these contributions, with the result that many people whom I should thank here will have to be content knowing that I really am grateful, even if, right at the moment, with my publisher breathing down my neck to write this, I am somehow overlooking various moments in the book's development. Don't be hurt. If it helps, know that a woman once called our house asking for Katherine, and after telling her repeatedly that no Katherine lived there, and please don't call back, I got off the phone only to have my wife remind me that Kate – her name – is short for Katherine. So my memory is not to be trusted.

With that caveat in mind, let me thank the following for their comments on early portions of the manuscript and/or their support in my efforts to complete it: Jon Adolph, Matt Andler, Fred Appel, Brian Baldi, Molly Bassett, Patrick Coby, Joan Cocks, Elizabeth Branch Dyson, Jim Emshoff, Catherine Epstein, Mike Evans, Ellie Faustino, Chris Jackson, Elizabeth Knoll, Joe Levine, Dan Levinson, Barrie Lindsay, Jan Lindsay, Meg Mott, Katherine Nelson, Billy Parker, Carol Rogers, Karen St. Claire, Austin Sarat, Carol Singer, Mary Dean Sorcinelli, Peter Struck, and Hannah Wild. To my mentor on all matters of teaching, Harry

Dangel, I owe a special debt of gratitude. Thanks also to Janice Evans, Doug Hildebrand, Jane Kelly, Lisa Jemison, Breanna Muir, and Meg Patterson at the University of Toronto Press, and to freelancer Barry Norris for his marvelous copy editing. My wife, Kate Binzen, and my children, Jake Binzen and Claire Lindsay, provided the love and support that kept me sane throughout. And last, but certainly not least, thanks to the participants in the educational workshops and seminars I've given over the years, and, of course, to thirty-five years of wonderful students at Georgia State University, Harvard University, the University of New Hampshire, the University of Toronto, Thayer Academy, Hancock State Prison, Lee Arrendale State Prison, Phillips State Prison, Walker State Prison, and the Atlanta Transitional Center. I learned more from them than they ever could have from me.

It is common practice to absolve the acknowledged of any responsibility for whatever errors might follow, and, to be sure, it was my decision to put them in the book. Still, I know I couldn't have come up with all of these errors on my own.

THE CRAFT OF UNIVERSITY TEACHING

Introduction: The Moments

Teaching Moments

Teaching Moment 1. Several years ago I received a rather unusual essay from a student in my classical political philosophy class. The essay was written as part of an in-class test, and it was in response to the following set of questions: "What is Aristotle's critique of Plato's ideal state? Who, in your mind, is making more sense here, Plato or Aristotle? Has Aristotle interpreted Plato correctly?" The essay, in its entirety, read as follows:

> Both Aristotle and Plato seem to enjoy using the "ideal state" as tools to guide the reader and instruct about complex subjects. Plato's ideal state is one of perfect harmony and balance that finds us wondering about its origins. It reminds me of a song by a man named Kenny Rogers, who coincidently just filmed a music video at my building. For some reason he was on the roof in his black trench coat singing about god knows what. You've got to know when to hold 'em, know when to fold 'em, know when to walk away, know when to run. The current state of country music is so poor that there aren't even any Kenny Rogers-esce singers anymore. For Christ sake, Buck Owens just died and that guy altered country music forever. To me the ideal state would have this moral support. The ideal state would have bingo and old people and cars that fly. And it damn well would have Kenny Rogers. Not Kenny Loggins though, god

knows that if that guy gets a career again we'll all have to hope lightning strikes our aunt Jessie's favorite adult contemporary station. Doesn't that stuff make you sick? It's like riding in the teacups at Disneyland after a 3-day bender.

If you are like me, you might at this point need to be reminded of something you've probably forgotten: the basic question at issue was, "What is Aristotle's critique of Plato's ideal state?" When I first read this essay, I didn't know really what to do with it. The essay had some obvious shortcomings, not the least of which was a singular lack of any knowledge of the subject matter. But I confess that what struck me more about it were its virtues. It was, for instance, one of the best-written essays I got, although part of that virtue was no doubt due to the fact that the author was not weighed down with the burden of having to express difficult philosophical ideas – or, for that matter, any philosophical ideas.

But it wasn't just well written, it was creative; it was amusing; it was engaging – it was a joy to read. I've probably read this essay twenty times, which means I've given it nineteen more reads than most other essays I've graded (twenty more than some). I also liked that the author made an attempt to do more than simply regurgitate ideas; he tried to relate the subject matter to contemporary life (although I admit the connections are tenuous at best). What I liked most about the essay, however, was the sheer honesty of it. This kid could have pulled off a D or C with the usual pabulum one gets in the know-nothing essay, and yet he chose not to go down that road. Here, for instance, is how another essay from the same class began: "Plato and Aristotle were two of the greatest men to come out of Greek civilization – one of the greatest civilizations to ever exist. They are the founders of all the modern philosophic paradigms – the giants upon whose shoulders all philosophers have since stood." The essay went on like this for paragraphs, or at least I think it did – I gave up after the author surpassed my superlative quota. But the thing is, this strategy – just start talking and hope for the best, a strategy we now call the Sarah Palin Technique – sort of works. The guy fumbled his way through a few pages, but because he managed, by sheer coincidence, to say a couple of correct things, I couldn't bring myself to give him a zero.[1] Instead he wound up with a D, a grade that, while bad, would not make it numerically impossible to salvage a decent grade in the course. (I did in my comments, however, write, "If Plato and Aristotle were so great, heck, why not buy one of their books?" In retrospect, this might have been a bit harsh.) The bottom line is that, if one reads enough of this second type of essay – essays that really waste your time and to which you somehow give a passing grade – one comes to appreciate the rare student with the courage to say, "Sorry, I didn't prepare. I have no clue what the hell I'm talking about. Here, however, are some thoughts on country music."

So those were the positives: well written, creative, honest.[2] But still, on the negative side there was that pesky fact that he hadn't said much – okay, *nothing* – about Plato or Aristotle. So, what to do? Complicating the matter was that two-thirds of the course remained. If I gave him a zero – which would reflect his knowledge of the subject matter – what would happen? Would he give up altogether, realizing that the best he could do in the course was a D? On the other hand, if I didn't give him a zero, would he reward me in future essays with more disquisitions on country music?

I went back and forth a lot here, and in the process of doing so eventually came to ask myself, perhaps for the first time in my teaching career, What am I trying to do with the grades I hand out? Are grades meant to be just a straight measure of the student's grasp of some body of knowledge? Is it true, to quote from a handbook for teachers, that "[t]he purpose of grades is to communicate the extent to which students have learned the course materials"? And if they are simply a measure of performance, can that measurement be made with respect to the other students, or does it have to be with respect to some objective benchmark? In an altogether different vein, is it possible to look at grades more broadly and holistically, as a means not just to measure learning, but to encourage it as well? And with that question in mind, might we use grades to reward improvement? Lots of questions, all in some way pointing to the one whose answer I was seeking: is there a philosophy of grading that could guide me in deciding what to do with this Aristotle-Kenny Rogers analysis?

Teaching Moment 2. When my son was about seven years old, we got a call from his teacher. She was upset with him. She reported that he had told a rather disturbing joke in class. The joke, she said, went like this: "Why did the dead baby cross the road?" Answer: "It was stapled to the chicken." Immediately I felt very uncomfortable, all the more so when she asked, "Where on earth would a seven-year-old learn a joke like that?" Embarrassingly I had to admit to her that I had in fact told him the joke myself. She seemed quite horrified at this prospect. Horror, at least, was the tone in her voice when she asked, "And do you think that's *funny*?!" I somewhat sheepishly replied that … well … *he* had certainly gotten a big kick out of it. She didn't sound impressed, so I moved into academic mode and tried to deconstruct the joke for her. I explained how it works on shock value – not only is the baby unpleasantly dead, it also has the misfortune of being stapled to a chicken. And even worse, it's also trying to get across a street, which is dangerous in any case (although, granted, it's dead). "*And*," I concluded, "all this is kind of funny in the context of the general banality of chickens-crossing-roads jokes. The joke works because these jokes are supposed to be cute, not sick and depraved."

There was silence at the other end of the line. I'm sure she was deliberating over her ethical responsibilities. Or perhaps she'd skipped that relatively short endeavor and was now looking up the number for child protective services. In the end she rather vaguely suggested that I keep age-appropriateness in mind when telling jokes to my children. (My first thought was that I *had* – *who*, after all, would enjoy this joke more than a seven-year-old? I kept this thought to myself, however.)

After hanging up, I found myself feeling grateful that I was not a second grade teacher; that, as a professor, I wasn't burdened with the sorts of ethical responsibilities that primary school teachers have, responsibilities that mandate telephone calls to parents, and – in extreme cases – to the nearest law enforcement. And then it dawned on me that that's not entirely so, that while perhaps I don't have to make painful phone calls to parents – in fact the law prevents me from doing so – I am hardly off the proverbial moral hook. As a university instructor, I don't face the *same* ethical issues and responsibilities as do primary and secondary instructors, but I clearly do face them. An obvious example quickly came to mind: what is the ethical thing to do when confronted with a student who seems emotionally or psychologically disturbed, a student who might be a danger to him- or herself or – worse – to others? For a primary or secondary school teacher, such a situation clearly imposes ethical responsibilities. But of course – as the tragedies at Concordia University and Virginia Tech illustrate all too vividly – it does for me as well.

The unstable student is simply at the extreme of a much larger ethical issue: when are we in any way ethically obligated to get involved in the private lives of our students? The answer is different for professors than it is for second grade teachers, but the question is no less ours. And the fact that our students are older actually *adds* ethical issues that aren't as apparent at earlier stages. What, for instance, are the limits of the relationship that we can have with our students? Is having a coffee okay? A beer? Many beers? (How many?) Can we ask them to babysit? And does our answer change with our different roles? After all, at this level, we're not just the students' teachers, we're also their mentors, their co-authors, their lab supervisors.

The more one thinks about life as a professor, the more apparent it becomes that our primary difficulty is not in trying to resolve the dilemmas we face; it's in trying to recognize when we're in them. Here's the rule of thumb I've come to accept: if I think I have a moral dilemma on my hands, then I do. If I don't think I have a moral dilemma on my hands, then I really do. If that sounds like an exaggeration, just consider how easy it is to come up with other examples. Can you offer a student a makeup exam if you haven't made that offer to her classmates? How many sides of an academic debate do you need to present? At what point does a laissez-faire thesis supervisor become a negligent one? How up-to-date on your subject matter do you need to be to teach it? How up-to-date on instructional methods do you need to be to teach *at all*?

To complicate matters, with each of these questions comes the issue of *whom* we have ethical responsibilities *to*. Consider the ubiquitous issue of academic dishonesty. Before we can figure out what our responsibilities are, we need to consider to whom we owe them. Do we owe them to the student who violated academic norms? Do we owe them to his or her classmates who did not? Do we owe them to our colleagues – to whom we might pass this student in the event we don't take action? Do we owe them to the institutions that employ us? To our academic discipline? To society at large? *To ourselves*?

Think about the medical professor who turns a blind eye to an academic infraction, thereby sending into the world an ethically and perhaps intellectually challenged doctor. Whose trust has the professor violated? It would be karma of the highest sort if, years later, that professor were wheeled into the operating room only to look up and see her former student. Admittedly the stakes are not usually this high – not all disciplines train their graduates for such vital services. The point, however, remains: it is awfully easy *not* to take formal action in cases of dishonesty. But then the question becomes: do you yourself – by your *in*action – violate academia's code of ethics?

You have, perhaps, seen a connection between these first two teaching moments. In fact, perhaps you've seen two. One I'll mention now, and one I'll come back to. First, consider that how I treat my Plato scholar is, while a pedagogical matter, also an ethical matter. For instance, encouraging him to stay in the class might involve treating him differently from his peers, which would raise the question of whether I could justify such treatment. And that, in turn, raises a broader question: is the ethically right thing to do necessarily the *pedagogically* right thing to do? Might there be times when the course of action that makes ethical sense would be disastrous pedagogically – or vice versa? What, in other words, is the relationship between pedagogy and ethics? The following might help.

Teaching Moment 3. This moment involves an ethical lapse of my own. A few years ago I had a graduate seminar that was not going at all well. The students had absolutely nothing to say and, consequently, relied on me to carry way too much of the conversation. Unfortunately I had nothing much to say either. My principal objective for the class had been reduced to the rather modest goal of staying awake. (It's so awful to be aroused from a nice doze only to find yourself in a bad class, one under your suspect leadership.) One day, as I sat in my office before class, it dawned on me that I'd rather slit my wrists than face this group. In fact, I thought that perhaps if I slit my wrists in front of them it might at least get them talking (although, with this group, even that wasn't a sure bet).

It was, in other words, a desperate situation. And here I should emphasize that it was also a rare one, at least with respect to my attitude. I love teaching, and I have a default fondness for my students. I readily accept that underperforming and seemingly lazy students very often have good reasons (often financial) to put their energies into non-academic pursuits. And even in the case of those prone to the worst of sins – incuriosity – my general perspective is that the responsibility for this unfortunate state in some way lies with me. (I'll say more about this in Chapter One.) That said, I can, like most educators, get frustrated, and I can also let that frustration darken my view of both what I am teaching and whom I am teaching. This desperate situation was one such occasion. And as desperate situations call for desperate measures, I right then and there made a desperate decision: *I wasn't going to go to class.* All I needed was some clever justification. Fortunately, as a political philosopher, I had a PhD's worth of training in dubious justifications, and sure enough, a few minutes later, I walked into the class and announced that we'd be doing something different that day. "I," I told them, "will today be stepping out and letting you talk amongst yourselves – *without me*." The reason, I explained, was that, as graduate students, they ought to wean themselves from the need for guidance. They were now at the point of their training when ideas should be discussed, not for *credit* (a word I enunciated with particular distaste), but because of their intrinsic intellectual worth. "You," I explained, "are now part of the academy. You are the few, the proud, the best, the brightest."

Admittedly I got a bit carried away, but the more I talked, the more moved I became. I even got a bit choked up. As for the students, they began to nod their heads in acknowledgment of the powerful wisdom of my words. And the more those words came, the more I also became convinced of their powerful wisdom. I almost forgot that this was really about my just wanting to get the hell out of there. Fortunately I snapped out of it and, true to my word, I left. I went back to my office, which was a bit down the hall. If I'd had a bottle of whiskey in my desk drawer, I'd have had a good stiff drink, just to add to the moral depravity. I had just skipped the first class of my teaching career.

Perhaps you can guess what happened next. My experience was very much like that of the Grinch listening to the Whos on Christmas morning: instead of witnessing dismay and confusion – or silence – I sat stunned as from across the hall wafted snippets of an intellectual discussion of the highest order. Oblivious to the fact that I could hear them, these students raised points I didn't think they were capable of. It was as if they were channeling Rousseau and Kant and Hegel. Just a week before, complete sentences had been well beyond them; at times I had suspected some were in a permanent vegetative state. But now, as I sat there, it dawned on me that *I* had been the problem in this class and that, through my moral depravity, I had hit upon a pretty effective pedagogical technique to overcome it.[3]

As one might imagine, I was eager to apply this newfound technique to all my classes. After all, if it's really about student learning, and if my students are really learning better without me, then perhaps a week skiing in the Alps would be to *everyone's* advantage – a win-win situation. To be sure, there might be limits to how far one could take this insight.

What interests me more than those limits, however, are the questions they raise: which limits should one be concerned with – the ethical or the pedagogical? and is it possible that the two might at times be in conflict? or is it the case that the ethical world circumscribes the pedagogical one, and that the pedagogically correct course of action could never be the ethically *in*appropriate one?

I said that two things connected the first two teaching moments. The first is this theme of the relationship between pedagogy and morality. The second connection is, in a sense, more basic: each of these moments (including the third) touches on two distinct levels of education. Most obviously, each touches on straightforward, practical teaching issues: how should we assess an essay? what special allowances can we offer an individual student? how does one turn around a suicidally somnolent seminar? when do we teach too much and when do we teach too little? In addition to such practical issues, these moments give rise to more abstract pedagogical questions: what is grading for? what is ethically responsible academic behavior? what is the relationship between that behavior and pedagogically sound practice?

We have, then, three discrete levels of reality: the actual teaching moment, the practical teaching issues that it involves, and the abstract pedagogical issue that the practical issues raise. All educators have experience at the first two levels. We all have had numerous teaching moments, and those moments, over time, have informed the manner in which we approach the practical issues of day-to-day teaching. And for most educators – at all levels – that's it. In fact, that's especially true in higher education, where people think of themselves as historians and mathematicians and biologists well before they think of themselves as teachers of history, mathematics or biology, let alone as educational theorists. For the most part, when professors think deep, abstract thoughts, they will be about history, math, and biology, not about teaching any of those things.

Since you are reading these words, teaching for you probably extends beyond both the moment and the practical concerns – it is also the object of reflection. And perhaps you think you know where I'm taking this: I'm going to tell you that such reflective beings as you are the few, the proud, the elite. But, of course, if you've been reading at all closely, you'll be reluctant to have me tell you that. And although I honestly think it's true, that, in fact, is *not* my message.

But before I spell that message out ...

Teaching Moment 4. A couple of years ago, a colleague in my department received the following email from one of her students:

Hello Professor!

I talked about this issue in class but I wanted to make sure that you will get this through email as well. I am going to be missing class from November 2nd (Friday) through November 13th (Tuesday). I understand that will mean I will be missing Nov 2, Nov 5, Nov 7, Nov 9, and Nov 12 from your class, which are quite a few days but I am hoping these will be excused.

I have attended every single class from this point on and I really do enjoy your class :), but unfortunately due to the *pageant* I will be unable to be present :(

Here is the actual link of my pageant site: [omitted]

I am contestant number [omitted]. The rest of the information will be on there, but the pageant itself requires all contestants to be there a week prior to the pageant, that way the contestants can rehearse and what not. [*We can only wonder what "what not" entails.*]

I also think I will be missing Exam #2 during my away time. When would you like for me to take the exam? Before I leave or after I come back?

Sincerely,

The future Miss VietnamUsa (hopefully) :)

[Her name]

Obviously this email raises a practical teaching matter: what does one do? I confess that I have a certain view of beauty pageants that leads me to regard this excuse much as I would one that read, "Dear Professor, I won't be able to get to class for the next week because I'll be stoned out of my mind." Perhaps I'm limited in some way, but I have difficulty seeing how a two-week paean to superficiality somehow constitutes grounds for missing five class periods and a major test. But the question is, can I really justify that judgment? *Is it true* that a beauty pageant is not a legitimate excuse? If so, what about it renders it inadequate? To answer that, we need to be able, at a general level, to distinguish an acceptable from an unacceptable excuse. But what litmus test do we have to do that?

Most of us, I think, go by the test akin to Justice Potter Stewart's pornography test. Stewart famously said that he couldn't define pornography, but he knew it when he saw it. And, basically, after all my years of teaching, that's about as advanced a theory as I have for judging excuses. I know a good one when I see one: brain surgery, meteor hit my home – these work for me. Tummy tuck, recreational sedation – these do not. The extremes are easy. (As one professor recently put it, "When you have someone's death certificate in your hands, you have to accept their excuse."4) What I've never really thought about, however, is the deeper question of what the salient issues are that distinguish the good from the bad excuses.

And this is where things go from ultra-practical, ultra-mundane to matters that have some real, abstract pedagogical interest. To know a good excuse from a bad one requires us to think long and hard about several things: what are the legitimate academic standards to which we should hold our students? what, in the context of a classroom, does fairness mean? to what extent are the private lives of students just that – *private*?

I can illustrate this last issue with the example of an email I received a year or so ago. The email had an attachment that, when I opened it, revealed an X-ray that I later discovered was of a bowel. Apparently it was not a happy bowel. Perhaps you're thinking that this bowel belonged to a student of mine, a student who, in sending me the X-ray, was documenting a medical problem that caused her to miss class. And you'd be almost correct. A student who had missed class did send this to me. But the weird thing about this bowel is that it did not belong to her. The X-ray was of her mother's unhappy bowel. And if that leaves you perplexed, then, well, you can appreciate how I felt. And I asked her: "So this is *not* the bowel that missed class?" It's odd how sometimes too much information can lead to too little understanding.

I wish I could, in the end, tell you why I was treated to this photo. Or, for that matter, to another one I received right after waking up one morning. This time the photo was of a student's leg, a leg that had what appeared to be blisters all over it. In my drowsy state, it was difficult to tell exactly what they were, and the experience served as a lesson not to open attachments from students at 7:00 a.m. I'm not all that squeamish, but I can assure you that my breakfast just didn't taste the same after viewing those blisters. What was interesting in this case was the idea that, in the student's mind, the photo constituted medical documentation for a class she'd be missing. The inference, I think, was that I am a medical doctor, and apparently a damn good one. She was not telling me that a doctor had documented that she had an aggressively unbecoming skin disease; she was looking for *my* medical judgment and, in the process, showing me far, far too much. (The condition had spread. There were other photos.)

We can all think of surgeries where this style of documentation would be completely inappropriate. I'm more than happy to accept on faith that a student has had a vasectomy or that sundry body parts are now augmented. Before and after photos will do nothing to strengthen that faith. But, to remind you of the issue here, does accepting one student's excuse – *on faith* – involve an inherent unfairness to another? Again, what does privacy mean in the context of education? And what does that meaning say about the nature of the student-faculty relationship?

◆

If we think again about our three levels – the teaching moment, the practical concerns, and the more abstract pedagogical reflection – it doesn't take much thought about each level, or about the relationship between them, to realize that educators are in a fascinating profession. The questions, the issues, the concepts – they're endless, and they're endlessly beguiling. I trust I don't need to convince readers of this fact. What I want to draw attention to instead is not how fascinating each level is, but how we think about them and, in particular, the relationship between them. The most commonly expressed thought about these levels is that we work through them in a sort of circular fashion: our classroom experiences inform the practical concerns that, in turn, inform the abstract reflection, and then we use the abstract to devise revised practices that, in the end, affect our classroom experiences. And then the cycle begins again.

In this circular vision, there is no ontological priority – just motion. We move between different pedagogical levels, each informing the next, and with each iteration we gain a richer understanding of the practice of education. Yet although we pay lip service to this notion of circularity, there is among educators a sense that there is something more noble about the abstract, a sense that it is of a higher order – that, to generalize, perhaps through gathering reams of data or by confronting established developmental theories, is to be scholarly, to be intellectual. We might not perceive the abstract as ontologically prior (few educators are Platonists in this regard), but it is at the very least – to substitute one vague philosophical term for another – *epistemologically* prior: we *know* education when we know it abstractly.

Of course, this fetish runs through all of academia. As one moves toward abstraction, be it from the applied to the theoretical sciences or, in my own field, from non-ideal to ideal theory, there's a sense in which one is seen to move from soft disciplines to the hard ones – a metaphor that, Freudians might argue, explains it all. We in academia are seduced by abstraction, by generalization. In truth most professors teach, and don't reflect overly abstractly upon it. But for those who do reflect, the

Holy Grail is, paradoxically, to remove oneself from the particular class-room and to focus only on the universal one. The task is to figure out not how to grade *this* paper but how *to grade*. Writers on teaching and learning are held in high esteem to the extent that their findings are thought to be true beyond their own classrooms.

I would not argue that such research is a bad thing to do. To the extent that an underlying truth might reveal itself, all educators stand to learn from it. What I want to suggest, however, is that, although we might covet abstract and general truth, there are also reasons to be wary of it or even, at times, to ignore it altogether. The most obvious such reason is with regard to those places where that pedagogical cycle breaks down. Certainly we can accept that particular classroom settings might be entirely non-generalizable. But what's also true, if less obvious, is that certain general truths might have no bearing on particular classroom settings. Often, in our daily teaching lives, the particular "truth" of the moment might be the truth we really need, even when it is in direct conflict with a "higher," generalized, capital-T Truth. Sometimes we just *know* the grade, we just *know* whether or not to accept the excuse, and we *know* how to resolve the ethical dilemma – and we know those things, not from a body of theory that informs us, but, rather, because something about the moment in which we find ourselves suggests an answer that is as true as it is unique.

What that observation points to is the real reason to be wary of abstract and general truth: it can too easily blind us to the real beauty that exists in education. I'm thinking of a beauty that resides not in the theories we might develop or even the practical wisdom we might come to. It's the one that resides in those moments when we get an essay like my student's Kenny Rogers analysis or when we get a glorious picto-rial excuse or when being driven to despair prompts us to try things that lead to deep learning – moments that we could never fully repro-duce or repeat and that perhaps we would never *want* to reproduce or repeat, moments that matter on their own, independent of whatever they might mean collectively, moments without which our more general observations would have no significance, no purpose, and certainly no meaning. To put the point otherwise, if education is *about* something in a general sense, it is, paradoxically, about the particular. It is about the moments.

The Craft of Teaching

"Okay, sure," you might be thinking, "but what about all those questions you just raised?" What *is* grading all about? When *are* excuses legitimate? How *should* professors meet their ethical obligations, and what *are* they? Are education and ethics necessarily complementary? Is this book merely a collection of stories – anecdotes from which no practical or theoretical lessons might be extracted? Let me clarify: whatever arrogance I might possess does not extend to the delusion that the collection of stories I have amassed over thirty-five years of teaching would really be of interest to anyone other than my immediate family members (whose patience would be sorely tested as well). More to the point: I do in fact intend to address and offer some reflections on the practical and theoretical aspects of education. (In Chapter Five, for instance, I examine in more depth the ethical issues I have raised here.) What I wish to make clear, however, is that practical and theoretical concerns – the educational puzzles that challenge us intellectually – although supremely interesting, are important only insofar as they succeed in bringing life and purpose to the events of the everyday. In my mind, there is no circularity here: all roads lead to the classroom.

Now, that's an assertion that perhaps not all will accept. As I mentioned, academia prizes (fetishizes, even) attempts to step back and speak to abstract truth. My difficulty with the priority is not that it embraces a flawed Platonic idealism over an Aristotelian materialism or even that it offers yet another foolish paean to mind over body (or matter or experience). Perhaps it does both, but my concern has more to do with what the perspective says, or rather what it does not say, about teaching. Implicit in the claim that the everyday matters only for the sake of the eternal is that the everyday is merely a means to an end. It is of instrumental value, but not also of intrinsic value. I object to this idea in the same manner that I object to the idea that writing is a mere means to literary criticism. In that instance, the inversion – the notion that writing exists for the sake of criticism – seems patently absurd. Criticism sheds light on writing, perhaps, but it is in precisely that sense that criticism is the means and writing is the end. Similarly we can see that educational theory sheds light on teaching, and is thus a means to improving it. And we certainly don't teach for the sake of theories about teaching. Either way of looking at the relationship, it seems awfully strange to view teaching as the means and theorizing about it as the end.

One might object here that this view overlooks the strength of the theorist's argument: universal (or at least generalized) truths do have an appeal. And, to dig deeper, this means/end distinction relies on a prior and disputable claim about what the end is. One could, after all, claim that another end is to understand something about the nature of things. From this perspective, particular writings are a means to understanding the nature of writing, and day-to-day teaching experiences are the means to understanding the nature of education. When the end is Truth, then, writing *does* exist for literary criticism and teaching *does* exist for educational theory.

With this clarification in mind, we must then ask about the end we have in mind when we say that the universal is secondary to the day-to-day. To see what it is, think about what literary criticism might *not* do for writing: help us to appreciate its beauty.[5] It might help us understand many things about it, but when it comes to our aesthetic judgment of, say, a Shakespeare sonnet or an O'Connor short story, it might have little or nothing to offer. I would make a stronger argument when it comes to educational theory: not only does it *not* help us to see the beauty of what can and does happen in classrooms; it might actively blind us to the fact that there is beauty – beauty that resides not just in the intimate relations or the epiphanic moments classrooms engender, but in the manner, the process, through which those relations and those moments arise. It might blind us, then, to the fact that teaching is, however else one might conceive of it, a *craft*.

In this regard, a comparison with science is helpful. The experiments that scientists conduct have functions: they seek to demonstrate and prove the existence of various phenomena. For the most part, we judge the value of science against that function. That said, I would argue that there is in much science a certain beauty: not the beauty of its objects – nature, the cosmos – but the beauty of the manner through which it lays bare and exposes those objects. It does something, but it can do that something in a way – with an elegance – that grabs our attention for reasons largely independent of its functional success. Thought of in this manner, science becomes a craft, an activity with aesthetic properties.

The same is true of teaching. The craft of teaching – its beauty – resides in *how* it does what it does. Many of the strategies teachers employ involve a level of inventiveness, creativity, and/or ingenuity that we can appreciate at an aesthetic level (many do not – I do not claim that *all* teaching is good craftsmanship). We still need to be concerned that whatever was done actually *worked* (I say more on what that would mean in Chapter One), but just as we would find some room to appreciate a beautiful handmade knife whose blade was not particularly sharp, we can say that the craft of teaching exists at a level beyond its function and that, in light of that fact, teaching, like the knife, can be viewed as being more than simply a means to some further end.

An example will help. Perhaps you were wondering how I handled the Plato-Aristotle-Kenny Rogers essay. If so, my first question is: why does what *I* did matter? I presume your interest is not in hearing the pedagogically correct response to the situation. Rather, I suspect you would like to hear about a response that you could then mull over. And I suspect that in your mulling you would not immediately ask if it worked, but instead judge it on grounds such as its creativity and inventiveness. And perhaps you would judge me as a teacher based on what you decided. In fact, you might not even think to ask if it worked. The effect it had on the student would be in the back of your mind, perhaps, but as a teacher you might be more interested in the craft: how did he take the tools of education and adapt them to fit this particular situation? And although part of your judgment might center on the science of education – did he motivate the student to learn? did he push the student to appropriately high levels of knowledge? – another part might also center on the craft, on the matter of how I took that science and that situation and *crafted* a response.

Such was the way I responded when I read this essay to a graduate pedagogy seminar and asked the students to come up with their own responses. They came up with several very good ideas, but one in particular stood out:[6]

> I'd invite the student to office hours and say something along the lines of: The exam you submitted, while entertaining and well written, did not answer the question asked and deserves a failing grade. However, I'm going to offer an alternative assignment so that you won't have a zero for one-third of your grade. You seem to enjoy creative writing, so the assignment is to write a ten-page dialogue between Aristotle and Plato as they attempt to compose a country song about the ideal state. This sounds like a joke, but I'm serious about this. In grading this, I will look for all the elements I wanted to see in your exam. This paper will replace the exam, but the highest possible grade you can receive is a C because that was the lowest grade among your peers on the exam. It would not be fair to them to allow you a second opportunity that would provide a higher score than they received.

There are, on a technical level, so many things to like about this response. It forces the student to "transfer" his knowledge of the subject to a realm beyond the immediate topic; it taps into the skills that he's already demonstrated (and so gives him confidence); it addresses the issue of fairness to the other students; it explains and justifies to the student its rationale;

and, perhaps most important, it provides him a way to stay in the class. I confess I was initially struck by none of those factors. What hit me instead was its sheer beauty – I cannot look at this answer without seeing an inventive and resourceful mind, one perhaps destined to create classrooms and courses that challenge the boundaries of what education is all about. I have no idea how this strategy would have worked with my student. At a certain level, though, that wouldn't be my primary – or at least my only – concern.

I am emphasizing teaching as a craft because I do not want the more general discussions that follow to be taken for more than I intend. They are designed only to stimulate thinking about *possibilities* – about what teaching looks like if it is approached in a certain manner. Rather than offer abstract Truth, I have only thoughts that *might* lead to particular moments in education. If there exists any universal statement lurking here, it is that the best educational practices emerge only when we see teaching as the craft that it is.

To be sure, such a vision is not readily apparent, as the push for ever-higher levels of abstraction is hardly the only force that seeks to instrumentalize teaching. Another comes in the form of a perspective, ubiquitous in faculty development and often articulated with no small amount of earnestness, that "it isn't about teaching, it's about *learning!*" The central insight here (and it *is* an insight) is that reform of higher education must begin with a shift in focus from what we – professors – do to what they – our students – do. We must, to quote from an influential article that helped get this ball rolling, move from the "instructional paradigm" to the "learning paradigm."[7]

Now, I have no great qualms about the general idea that the purpose of education at any level is to produce learning, not teaching, and that the latter is, ultimately, a means to the former. Certainly this shift in perspective offers a helpful heuristic devise, one that ensures that we remain open to various alternative pedagogical strategies and that we assess education in a meaningful way.[8] Yet in the rush to airbrush teaching out of mission statements in favor of student learning, we forget that teaching is – *in addition* to being a means to learning – an activity worthy of attention in its own right. I'm not suggesting that teaching can be judged without reference to learning – it is emphatically true that, if our students have not learned, then we have not taught, however valiantly we might have prepared our syllabi, delivered our lectures, or assessed our students' work. (I will, however, qualify that remark later.) Reduced to an abstraction, teaching might indeed be about nothing more than learning. That said, we *can* talk about – even focus on – teaching without bringing on the devastating consequences linked to the instructional paradigm (and they are legion).[9] I would go further still and suggest that many of the changes envisioned by "learning" advocates might best be promoted if professors were allowed to think long and hard about what it is they do. To presume otherwise is to be overly enamored of an academic culture that says "it's all about learning," but that has somehow forgotten what learning is all about.

But this perspective is not the greatest threat to the idea of teaching as a craft – far from it. Any views we have of teaching take hold only to the extent that they resonate within a larger social context, and so we might understand all tendencies to downplay the craft of teaching as part of something larger. Indeed, one need not look far to see that the inversion of teaching from an end to a means is *itself* a moment, one embedded firmly within a broad assault on anything that smacks of intrinsic value. In truth, the fate of teaching is really no different than the fate of all crafts: it too is now a commodity. As a commodity, it is increasingly called upon to generate measurable (and marketable) "learning outcomes," while its practitioners are rated online so as to make consumer choice in education as "rational" as it is in, say, the automobile and computer markets. Of course, one could say that teaching has always been a commodity, yet it seems undeniable that, in an era of vanishing education budgets and online outsourcing, its commodification has a contemporary flavor to it. (There might be an art to online teaching, but it is a stretch to think that its explosion stems predominantly from a desire for new forms of pedagogical expression.) Even where teaching is downright fetishized, as it is in the American No Child Left Behind and Race to the Top initiatives, it isn't the craft that is held in esteem, but rather the teacher's ability to transform students into vessels of testable knowledge.[10]

In short, if it is easy to conceive of teaching as a mere instrument, it is because the same can be said for education as a whole. Indeed the instrumentalization of teaching runs hand in hand with the instrumentalization of learning, with the perception of knowledge itself as a mere means, something to be acquired solely for a job or money or prestige or power or security or identity or – well – anything else. Knowledge, like a university degree, must be put to use and, as such, cannot stand as the object of a young person's desire. In this climate, education is consumed by students (the consumers) whose motivation to learn – *to know* – gradually gives way to more pragmatic desires: to be a lawyer, a doctor, an engineer, a banker.

It is in such an environment that teaching as a craft becomes an act of rebellion. It wages battle not against knowledge itself; it does not deny students the skills they require for their careers. (Responsible education should always have an eye to the future persons that students become.) Rather, the rebellion in this case is against the instrumental manner in which students increasingly come to hold knowledge. Hence a teacher working to preserve her craft's intrinsic value will of necessity promote the intrinsic value of learning and, in so doing, oppose the kind of teaching that has no concern with *how* and *why* students come to the knowledge an education can provide. In this respect, the craft of teaching entails an art of knowing, an art in which the very distinctions we make between teaching and learning begin to blur, one in which teaching and learning, at present two distinct moments in education, aim at collapsing into one.

It is, at least, to such a proposition that I now turn. In what follows, I argue that teaching as an endeavor looks, from the perspective of the teacher, different when it is undertaken as a craft. Chapter One explores this claim at its most general level, asking what teaching as a craft means with respect to the end – the ultimate goal – that we set for ourselves. In Chapter Two, I argue that, from the perspective of a craft, the success of the learning experiences we create is determined less by what we do than by who we are. In Chapter Three, I dispel any notions that craft teaching is about personality – here I look at how much teaching we can do simply by thinking long and hard about the readings we assign. Then, in Chapter Four, I turn to technology, a force whose power to destroy the craft element of teaching rivals any others. Finally, in Chapter Five, I examine the breakdown of the learning environment, asking what such an event means from a craft perspective and how, from that perspective, we might conceptualize solutions.

In short, what follows is an account of how a change in the way we approach teaching colors anything and everything we as professors do. My account is, of course, meant only as a start – there will always be more to write. Such, I hope to show, is the nature of a craft.

What Is Craft Teaching?

The issue is not to teach him the sciences but to give him the taste for loving them and methods for learning them when this taste is better developed.

– Jean-Jacques Rousseau[1]

The general principles of any study you may learn by books at home; but the detail, the colour, the tone, the air, the life which makes it live in us, you must catch all these from those in whom it lives already.

– Cardinal John Henry Newman[2]

To be a teacher is, above all, to let others learn.

– Martin Heidegger[3]

Crafts

Many academics can point to a particular moment when they fell in love with their discipline. In my case that moment came while reviewing study questions for an undergraduate exam in the history of political philosophy. The topic was Marx, in particular his *Economic and Philosophic Manuscripts of 1844*. One of the questions was on the role of money in capitalist society. As my study group discussed possible answers, it suddenly dawned on me that, in Marx's mind, money – "the alienating ability of mankind"[4] – had become us (or we it). It was not just that money, as any casual observer of the rich and famous will attest, can "transform all my incapacities into their contrary."[5] What really struck me – what *excited* me – was Marx's explanation of how this situation had come to be: in the wage relationship, we lose the ability to see ourselves in what we do and, as a result, come to see our essence in the paycheck we receive. We now *are* that paycheck. As he put it, in characteristically enigmatic terms, "[w]hatever the product of his labor is, he is not. Therefore the greater this product, the less is he himself."[6]

What Marx pushed readers like myself to consider was that this state of affairs might be otherwise – that, for our productive efforts, we might, were conditions of work transformed, see not money, but *ourselves*. Our work might yield not (just) a paycheck, but the extension of those selves. Work would be a means to creative expression, an expression of who we were. Here was a vision of human life that seemed, to my twenty-one-year-old self, true in some irrefutable sense – a vision that, as I began to devour other works of political philosophy, just kept making more and more sense, such that, three decades later, it appears to be one I will never quite shake. As a political philosopher, I am still driven to reflect on why I should believe my (or any) life has much meaning, and why that meaning might be wrapped up in what we do, and how, in the process, we express ourselves. (That Marx would have scoffed at the possibility of creative, meaningful production within a market society was a detail that, over time, troubled me less and less.)

Looking back on this learning experience and the many that followed, I am struck by a coincidence: my Marx-inspired pursuit of a creative, unalienated life led me to a career focused on trying to create such experiences for others. As soon as I began teaching, I became consumed by the idea that, for every student I taught, there was a Marx-like event waiting always to happen. Whether the moment was with Marx or Plato or Adam Smith didn't matter; I certainly don't (consciously) push any particular ideas on my students. What I do push is the possibility that, at any given moment, *some* idea might sweep over them as this idea of Marx's swept over me.

What really mattered to me those many years ago had, then, little to do with Marx. What mattered was that at twenty-one I was sitting in a friend's apartment with a set of questions that a professor had given us, preparing for a test he had structured on readings he had chosen. In looking back, I wonder how that professor had come to make the decisions that resulted in my sudden inspiration. What thoughts lay behind the questions he chose? Were they drawn from points he had made in class? Were they meaningful only in virtue of questions he had chosen on previous tests? And what about the prior decisions to assess us with in-class essays or to use study questions as a guide? Or even the readings themselves: why *that* particular work of Marx? I will never know how much credit for my experience this professor is really due – perhaps many of his choices had been made with no pedagogical considerations in mind – but what I do know is that that experience came from a set of conditions that professors, with varying degrees of intention, can and do create. Indeed *all* educational experiences, the good and the bad alike, are acts of creation. Like writing a novel or making furniture or building a house, constructing learning experiences demands creative powers and, as such, leads to a result that bears the imprint of those creative powers. As one can look at a painting and see in it the embodiment of the artist ("that's a Miró!"), one can look at learning experiences and their participants, and in each one see the mind behind it: "That's a so-and-so test." "Those are so-and-so's students." One can see, in other words, that the construction of learning experiences is, above all else, a craft.

At least it can be. A craft, on my understanding of it, has both objective and subjective elements. The former, in the case of teaching, involve the activities I've just described: taking the tools of education – lectures, discussions, syllabi, assignments, methods of assessment – and "crafting" experiences that lead to learning. In addition to hard work and discipline, such activities require inventiveness, ingenuity, a sound knowledge of fundamental principles – to name a few obvious requirements.

They also involve conditions that determine how free the craftsperson is to create a learning environment bearing his or her imprint. In the worst cases, where the terms on which we teach are not our own (where we are handed a syllabus, tests, lectures, notes, course objectives, and told: *Teach!*), the process and the end result, far from reflecting our creative powers, confront us in a strange and often hostile manner: they are not *us*, and we, whoever we are, are no longer engaged in a craft.

It is not enough, however, to wield the tools of education in the manner we decide. Craft production is also a subjective matter. Put simply, it needs to be approached with a certain attitude. Even when it involves – as it always does at some point – a given amount of drudgery, it must also, and *always*, be an activity carried out with the conscious desire for self-expression.[7] The process and the result must confront the craftsperson as an expression of herself, one she accepts – happily, disappointedly, with pride or with embarrassment – as the embodiment of her creative powers. Moreover the confrontation itself must be intentional and deliberate: we must continually reflect on what we do – on the learning environments we create and on the students whom we create with them. In this respect, of all the people who see in an assignment or a classroom activity the embodiment of the teacher, the most important is the teacher herself.

These objective and subjective elements clearly have great effects on one another. Acts of conscious self-expression are far harder to come by when our activities are constrained from above. Likewise the attitude we have in approaching an activity will have much to say about the goals we set and the means by which we choose to arrive at them. In what follows, however, I focus only on the subjective element, not because the objective is unimportant or unrelated, but because – irrespective of the tools at our disposal and the conditions in which we find ourselves – our attitude toward what we do will *always* be relevant; it will always make a difference in the degree to which the activity is a craft. We might have to teach a curriculum not of our choosing, or to the standards of an accrediting body or licensing board, but the perspective we take on these tasks – this subjective moment in our activity – is, I would argue, the central component of teaching as a craft.

Stripped to its essentials, the idea is as follows: we teach as a craft when we teach as a creative activity – one through which we seek to express ourselves. This understanding of a craft might strike some as overly broad and somewhat elusive, or worse, not in keeping with their own understanding. For now, though, I'll leave it at that. My hope is that if you aren't clear on it by now, you will be in ten, twenty, or a hundred pages. And if you *are* clear on it, perhaps you'll have a different idea when you get to the end. I don't, in any case, think that it would make pedagogical sense to try to *define* craft or craft teaching; better to take time and *show* it to you. Slowly. In a sense, this entire book is a meditation on what *I* think it means teach as a craft, one designed to persuade you that it might be a good thing to understand teaching in this manner. This overview, sparse as it is, has just been to get us started – to help you to make some sense of what follows. If all I have done thus far is to elicit in you another, perhaps more sophisticated understanding of a craft, so be it – I would welcome learning about it.

I do think that what little I've said thus far already offers a sharp contrast to what teaching in higher education has become for many of its practitioners. More important, I think it also points to a different way to approach teaching. And here I don't mean simply that if you think what you're doing reflects on you and, more urgently, reflects on a constitutive aspect of you – if you think, in other words, that it goes to the core of your being and defines who you are – then you'll treat it with care and, as a result, probably do it better. The issue isn't just doing what we do more conscientiously or better. It is that the *goal* of our efforts – the *end* toward which our efforts are directed – might, when viewed from a craft perspective, appear different altogether.

So what do I mean by that statement? How does the goal of teaching change when we come to see our efforts as a reflection of ourselves? I have suggested the answer already, but to make it clearer, take a moment and think about the great teaching experiences that you've had, the ones that made you feel an especially strong sense of accomplishment and fulfillment. I'm serious about this request, and not just because it will help to make my point conceptually. I'm serious because it makes sense pedagogically. I want to express my thoughts in a pedagogically sound manner, and such a manner requires a fairly regular use of concrete examples. In this instance I could supply examples – of *my* fulfilling teaching experiences – but what follows will be far more meaningful to you (hence the pedagogical soundness) if we start with an experience in your head rather than in mine.

So, before reading on, think for a moment. What experiences in the classroom have you had that felt really good – in the sense of providing a feeling of personal fulfillment? Shut the book and think about it for five minutes. And while you're at it, think about bad experiences, too – the ones that, in confirming every suspicion that you were indeed a fraud, made you rue the day they gave you a job teaching.

(I suppose I could break from the discussion and tell you a story while you think. But then you would be thinking of that story. That is, if it were a *good* story. Perhaps, to get you thinking about your teaching moment, I should tell you a *bad* story – one that would allow you to think about something else. Or better yet, I could give you a bad lecture. There is nothing quite like a bad lecture to inspire people to great thinking – in fact, it is entirely underrated as an occasion to sort out your worldly problems. You can think and learn about so much during a bad lecture, although, granted, not about anything concerning the lecture itself, the subject of which might be the only one to which your mind does *not* go. It certainly can't be said that a bad lecture doesn't lead to learning, though. Or at least it *couldn't* be said – these days, the cell phone and laptop computer have diminished the virtues of a bad lecture, as they no longer allow our mind to drift where it wants to drift but lead us straight to places – through texts or postings or chats that teach us nothing except perhaps that our friend Cindy really is breaking up with our other friend Brad – from which there is no possible return to the lecture that sent you packing in the first place.

Doodling in a notebook at least offered a return trip to the classroom. Texting is a one-way ticket to anywhere but where you're sitting. But I'm getting ahead of myself here. For now, put the book down, and think about those teaching experiences.)

Now, with those experiences in your head, start with the good ones, and think specifically about the products of those experiences: a certain class or perhaps an individual student. Then move on to the bad ones, the ones that got away: the class you dreaded or the student who left your classroom no better off than when she arrived. In either case let me venture a guess about the characteristics that do *not* distinguish these two very different scenarios. Their defining feature is *not* that the student came away having far more or, in the worst-case scenario, far less, knowledge. At a minimum I would wager that the student's having learned a lot or very little was not what made the image come to mind. Sure, there might have been a student who came to your class woefully unprepared and, after struggling mightily for the first few weeks, gradually came to "get it" – so much so that, by the end, she achieved a level of knowledge she would not have imagined possible at the outset. Or perhaps there was a class that really jelled as a group and, with your support and guidance, created an intellectually vibrant environment in which all its members displayed incredibly rapid improvement. My guess is that, if you really think about these experiences, though, you'll see that behind this increase in knowledge – indeed, at the root of it – was a change in *attitude* about knowledge, about learning.

And this point gets at the characteristic that, I wager, *does* distinguish your dream and your nightmare visions: they created, respectively, a surfeit and a deficit, not of learning, but of *enthusiasm* for learning. In the positive scenario, what filled you with pride was that your students seemed so exuberant to learn – just as, in the negative one, it was their complete lack of interest, their boredom, that was so distressing, and that, quite probably, lay at the root of the disrespectful behaviors so vividly etched in your mind years later. At some level, then, we recognize that at the core of success in teaching lies not the acquisition of knowledge or even learning itself, but the creation of enthusiasm about knowledge and about learning.

As widely shared as this understanding of success in teaching might be, it is not always a conscious understanding. I asked that you merely envision successful and unsuccessful experiences, rather than formulate a general definition of success, to get only at your intuitions. As a conscious, *reflected* matter, people tend to view success in teaching, and thus its goal, as being about transferring knowledge. The purpose is to give students those things – the skills, aptitudes, and body of knowledge – that we require for success in the tests we later give. Teaching is thus seen in a circular manner, or perhaps as an exchange: we transfer to students, and they, on the appointed day, transfer back to us.

On the craft view, the goal of teaching captures our intuitions about enthusiasm rather than these more reflected views. Craft teaching might employ the same tests, but not to see the learning *return*; on the contrary, when teaching is about generating enthusiasm for learning, the goal is for the student to take what she learns away from and beyond the class, in a direction and to a place only she can determine. The learning might come back temporarily on a test or a paper, but it cannot be deposited and left there. Craft teaching requires that learning leave the classroom – it must escape for anything to have been truly taught.

How does this view of teaching as the generation of enthusiasm about learning follow from the craft perspective? Think back to what I said earlier about professors. We who teach once found ourselves in educational experiences that started us down a road to becoming academics. We were inspired – to continue our studies, to teach ourselves (as all graduate students must) the subjects that now concern our professional lives. I would suggest that this formative experience has never left us. In fact, as your examples of teaching success already might have demonstrated, it remains at some level the basis for our judgments about education. The trick is to make that level a conscious one, a trick we would readily accomplish were we to reflect, as craft teaching demands we must, on the learning experiences through which we express ourselves as teachers. These experiences – in particular, the students they create – embody our craftsperson selves. They are us. Is it any wonder, then, that, when we envision the students we wish to create, we find ourselves staring at younger versions of ourselves?

In this sense craft teaching is an act of self-expression in two ways. We consciously and intentionally create learning experiences that express our own unique way of doing things (experiences that others might recognize as ours) and, in the process, we aim to create the same excited young students we once were. Craft teaching thus involves an odd case of self-replication, as we endeavor to create people who, like ourselves, are driven to teach *themselves*.

Objections

Enough grandiose talk. Surely there are objections to the idea that teaching is not at all about the transfer of knowledge, but about creating the conditions in which students become enthusiastic about knowledge? One obvious concern can be expressed as follows. Yes, teaching must leave students' motivational states altered, but if it does not alter other states as well, students will lack the capacity to follow their newfound muse. Motivation is required for further learning, but without changes to knowledge, beliefs, and so on – in the words of Ken Bain, the "intellectual and personal changes that people undergo as they develop new understandings and reasoning abilities"[8] – motivation could just lead to frustration. To get technical, people need to experience "a relatively permanent change in a neuron," or, to be yet more precise, a systematic change in "the synaptic potential of a neuron [– that is,] the likelihood of a neuron transmitting an electrical impulse."[9] Any and all such fantastic things must occur for a student to carry learning forward into the future, and many teachers are good precisely because they know how best to bring them about. Teaching, then, cannot be about *just* motivating.

I readily accept such claims about learning, but I don't think they undermine the view of teaching as that which attends *solely* to the motivation people need to get there. To tie teaching to the amount of knowledge acquired, the duration of time it is retained in the hippocampus, or the neural changes thereby created does not get at *how* we hold that knowledge, whatever its volume – although retention might be a good proxy for that, as I discuss in a moment. The part of learning that interests me as a teacher is the knowledge students hold *excitedly*. Yes, I want students to have the tools to continue their studies – new understandings and reasoning abilities; different beliefs, behaviors, or attitudes; greater synaptic potential – but mostly I just want them *to continue*. The particular beliefs, behaviors, and attitudes I prize are not those that allow for further study, but those that make it an irresistible fate.

There are two general defenses of this position, one that focuses on the close connection between motivation and learning and one that focuses on the effect of *believing* that this connection exists. I explore the latter defense in the next section, but let me start here with the connection itself. The most obvious thing to say is that very little learning happens without motivation. Indeed, it borders on a truism to say that the emotional state of excitement (about something) leads to motivation, and that motivation is essential to learning.[10] If, as Ambrose et al. argue, "learning is not something done *to* students, but rather something students themselves do,"[11] then much will depend on their own volition. It is precisely because I agree so emphatically that learning is something students do that I want to preserve for teaching only the task of convincing them to do it. After all, giving oneself new understandings and reasoning abilities is an immensely arduous endeavor – without a will to do it, there will be no way. As Shell et al. put it, "[i]f learning was effortless, we wouldn't need teachers or schools."[12] Teaching, then, is what aims to making learning effortless. One might complain that teaching so understood would be *before* and *temporally distinct* from learning. I could agree; I just wouldn't complain.

The irony here is that teaching becomes an activity whose goal is to make itself superfluous, or at least to make sure that learning is not forever contingent upon it. We want, as the cliché goes, to create "life-long learners." This thought provides a second link between motivation and learning: motivation not only kick starts learning, it determines its duration. Just as learning begins with the motivation, it ends when the motivation stops. Poor teaching (on this understanding of teaching) creates four-year (or in the case of my university, 6.1-year) learners; good teaching makes for classes that last fifteen years instead of fifteen weeks. In one sense of teaching, then, the better I do it, the *less* it will be directly connected to the knowledge students acquire, as they will be acquiring it years after they have forgotten my name. In another sense, however, a student who is still reading political philosophy fifteen years after taking my class is one that I am still teaching.

The final thing to say about the relationship between motivation and learning is that in some respects it is not a relationship at all – the two, rather, are indistinguishable from each other. Think here of learning in its most abstract sense: it is, above all, about change – change to our personal epistemology. But what happens when that change occurs? When we integrate external stimuli into that epistemology in such a way as to alter it, what is really going on inside our heads? A quick answer is that two processes are under way. In the first, we "practice" with whatever it is we have been taught – in the literal sense of playing an instrument, but also in memorizing material, solving problems, analyzing concepts – and when we do, neurons fire and, if fired frequently enough, grow and extend toward other neurons, thereby making connections that allow signals to be transported (via synapses). The whole process is actual physiologic change in the form of cellular growth.[13]

The second process is what interests us here. The change that learning brings about also involves an emotional component expressed in the brain through the release of chemicals such as dopamine, adrenalin, and serotonin. As Zull explains, "[w]hen our network connections are awash with emotional chemicals, synapse strength is modified and the responsiveness of neuron networks can be dramatically changed."[14] The conclusion he draws? "We must find ways to make learning intrinsically rewarding. Learning should feel good, and the students should become aware of those feelings."[15] We need, in other words, to motivate students to want to learn, and we need to do it not just because it will *lead* to learning, but because motivation entails the sort of emotional response that, neurologically speaking, *is* learning. Simply being excited to learn is learning.

I am, in the end, deeply sympathetic to the concern that a thoughtful critic of mine voiced in the following manner: "I do not want to create enthusiastic, ill-trained mathematicians."[16] My response is neither would I; for my part the prospect of creating enthusiastic, ill-trained political philosophers does not make me at all happy. That they are at least enthusiastic in their ignorance is of no consolation to me. Try as my critic and I both might, however, every year students *will* leave our classes ill-trained, and so the question is how might we best minimize that occurrence? I claim that focusing on enthusiasm is not simply a good way to ensure *enthusiasm*, but the best way to avoid *ill-training*. Thus, even on the view of teaching as the transfer of knowledge, a focus on motivation makes practical sense. In fact I would go further here and suggest that, if anything gets in the way of the transfer of knowledge, it is our singular attention to that transfer. It is to this proposition that I now turn.

Applications

General Considerations

Why go so far as to say that teachers need to focus on motivation *alone*? Why would teaching not be both motivating *and* transferring knowledge? The answer leads to the real defense of teaching as motivating, one that shifts the focus from what *students* do (learn) to what *teachers* do (teach). My thought here is that teaching conceived of only as motivating students to learn leads to practices, and the sort of perspective, that stand a better chance of promoting learning than does teaching conceived of as transferring knowledge – which, at the end of the day, might undermine learning altogether. So what are those practices?

It might help if I gave a couple of examples of what can happen when instructors shift their attention away from the transfer of course content and focus instead on motivation. Perhaps the most significant change that might occur has to do with the sheer volume of knowledge that many professors feel obligated to cover. Often, in discussing ways in which colleagues might enliven their classes, I hear the following complaint: "How can I possibly do what you're suggesting and still cover all the material?" This complaint usually leads to the following exchange:

LINDSAY: "Why do you need to cover so much material?"
COLLEAGUE: "Because it's in the curriculum."
L: "So the students need to know it?"
C: "Right."
L: "Could the students ever learn it without your covering it?"

This last question gets the conversation rolling, as it focuses attention on the relationship between the passive "the curriculum must be covered" and the active "I must cover the curriculum." The passive is true, but the active does not logically follow from it. In fact the passive statement is perhaps the best reason to reject the active. There is, at least, no necessary connection between the two, and it is highly probable that the more we cover the material in class, the less inclined students will be to cover it on their own outside class. Why? Because the more knowledge we seek to impart, the less able we are to do so in a pedagogically interesting manner, and, as a result, the less likely students are to impart it by themselves later.

It never ceases to surprise me how shocked professors are to consider that they do not need to cover all, or even most, of the material in their courses – and how liberated they feel. My standard advice is that, if there are five sections in Chapter Sixteen, pick the two that lend themselves best to interesting case studies and/or lucid, example-filled explanations – and run with them. To the objection that "I can't ignore the other three," I raise the passive/active distinction: "You're right, the other three *cannot* be ignored, but you might have to do just that. Your task is to cover the two chosen sections in such a manner as to make your *students* – not you – want to cover all five. Make them leave your class running to the library or the bookstore to read what you have willfully ignored. When learning stops with the ringing of the class bell or, worse, about forty minutes earlier, very little has been taught."

At this point I ask a few more basic questions: "Why were you covering the material in the first place? If you assigned a reading on it, one that you chose for its educational virtues, why did you feel the need simply to repeat it?" Answers generally take one of two forms: "I can't assume they've read it" or "I can't assume they fully understood it." (A third response – "I'm not sure; I never thought about it" – is also fairly common.) Both answers offer seemingly rational justifications for covering the material in class. (There would certainly be no excuse for covering the material if we assumed that the students had read and understood it.) The problem is not that instructors have failed to recognize the problem – be it non-reading or non-understanding – but that they have misjudged the cure.

Consider instances when students ignore or reject the reading. The knowledge we want them to acquire is out there, in the texts, yet when the students walked into class they had not seen fit to avail themselves of it. That fact contains important data. It suggests the problem isn't cognitive or conceptual or analytic, but motivational – weakness of will. With that understanding in mind, the task in the classroom is to do battle with apathy, not ignorance – and although coverage is not the weapon of choice in either case, it is especially counterproductive in the former.

But what about instances when students tried to tackle the reading but simply found it too difficult to grasp? Wouldn't coverage of the material be warranted here? My only reply is to ask whether the problem lies with the students or with the reading – the one *you* the professor chose. In other words, is the answer really that we should cover the material *not* learned or that we should choose a text from which students *can* learn? The point is crucial: teaching as motivating rejects coverage in part because it so emphatically demands meticulous considerations regarding the work we assign *outside* class. That work, too, must motivate – a point I discuss in greater detail in Chapter Three.

Of course, there might be cases where we've misjudged the reading – an error of which I am especially guilty – and here, it seems, the advice to choose readings wisely comes too late. In addition, for those of us who teach canonical historical texts, there is the fact that some of those texts are *not* pedagogically sound. Surely in these cases we can – must, even – cover the material that needs covering, no?

No. We want students to learn the material, but it is highly doubtful that the most effective means to that end is to cover it in its *entirety*. Such doubts stem from the same central point I've been stressing: the more we convey knowledge, the less likely students will convey it to themselves. If, then, we have a block of material that they need to know – an assumption all too often accepted without reflection – and a text that is causing difficulty, the best solution is still to spend the class motivating students to take another crack at it or perhaps even to find alternatives or supplements to the text. We can certainly aid them in that quest – pointing them to various resources, including, and especially, each other – but the quest must always be *theirs*, not ours. I am not suggesting that particular points cannot be explained in class, only that we choose these points not with an eye to comprehensiveness, but with consideration for the work students do when they leave class: What points might render that work clearer, more enjoyable, and – as a result – more likely to occur?[17]

My warning about coverage is often not an easy sell, but to the truly resistant I offer one bit of conclusive evidence: you actually know about the dangers of coverage already. In fact, you're already teaching with this insight in mind. You can prove it to yourself by looking over your past few years of lecture and seminar notes. I *guarantee* you will discover that you covered less and less material each time you taught the course. Perhaps you're on to something. (If they are new to teaching, I suggest they ask their more experienced colleagues about any changes *they* have observed.)

It is for good reason that "coverage is the enemy of understanding" is a well-worn adage in faculty development. What I am suggesting here is the reason it is so true: covering less frees up time to cover *creatively* – to press for active student involvement. Substantively it allows time to focus on what makes a subject worthy of attention, on aspects of a discipline that motivate learning because they challenge thought. When we cover less, we make time for students to apply, compare, evaluate, synthesize, and create knowledge, instead of simply naming, defining, locating, recognizing, or describing it. Covering less allows us, in short, to *teach*.[18]

My second example of a good thing that might happen if teaching were limited to generating enthusiasm has to do with a change not in tactics but in attitude. Any instructor who has ever spent time around a department water cooler will be familiar with the somewhat tiresome remark that "students are so ill-prepared these days; they never do the reading, and all they want is for me to spoon-feed them." Sometimes added are wistful allusions to the halcyon days when students were all prepared, eager, and respectful. The problem with this sentiment – other than its being historically challenged[19] – is that it allows faculty to put the blame for poor learning on students: *they* don't do what we ask. I am not denying that the sentiment often captures truth; I would only point out that that truth is interpreted very differently when we focus on teaching as motivating students. If our task is *only* to motivate, then ill-prepared students have not failed either us or themselves; it is we who have failed them. Yes, they did not prepare, or read, take notes, or even pay attention in the lectures; they often skipped class. I don't deny their agency. I would suggest, however, that none of these things happens in a vacuum; they happen, rather, because we did not motivate the students to do otherwise. In a world where teaching is motivating, water cooler conversations about the poor state of students become admissions of teaching failure.

Before you reject this idea out of hand, consider that, at the most basic level, it is a truism. To resort to philosophy-speak for a moment: if person A doesn't do what we want her to do (call it x), it is because of all the choices A has in her life, x did not win. To be sure, A might truly have *wanted* to do x (that is, she might have had some motivation to do x), but the fact that she did not do so reflects the further fact that some other choice (say, y) was more attractive: her motivation to do y exceeded her motivation to do x. My claim, then, is simply a description of reality, albeit a grossly simplified one, as I'm leaving aside the internal machinations – the causal attributions, outcome expectancies, and cognized goals – that affect the choices we make.[20]

Let me quickly address another objection you might have: "Suppose y was going to the hospital to get her broken arm repaired? Can we really say we've failed because she did not choose x?" My response is that, in such a case, A made a wise choice. I am not arguing that our students will always do, or *should* do, what we want them to do, only that our job is to work as hard as we can to motivate them to do so. The fact that the array of alternatives to x is vast and alluring – in other words, that the competition is stiff – in no way changes the task at hand. It simply makes it a greater challenge. In many cases, when our students don't learn, it is not because we have not done all we reasonably could, but because the alternatives or impediments to learning – whether virtuous (caring for a dying relative), not so virtuous (gluing oneself to a bong), or somewhere in between (the ubiquitous distractions of technology, a poor level of university preparedness, a growing sense of entitlement – pick your favorite villain) – proved insurmountable. No matter. As these factors are largely outside our control, there is not much we can do about them. What's important is that, when we fail, we can say that at least we did our best or perhaps all we could reasonably do. I am not suggesting there is any shame in many of the instances where we didn't motivate students to learn. I am simply saying that the mere fact of our not succeeding at the tasks we set for ourselves is not evidence that we set the wrong tasks.

If this discussion returns you to the thought that motivating students to learn (bringing A to x) seems like an awful responsibility, keep in mind that, on this model of teaching, it is the *only* responsibility we bear: we only need to get them excited. As for imparting knowledge, that's for the students to do (upon themselves) – although it is certainly up to us to hold them accountable, via various methods of assessment, to that task. I'm not sure if this is less or more work; it is, however, different work. More important, it is work *for us*. To dwell on what the students do or do not do is to focus on the action or inaction of others. If instead we direct our frustration *inward*, it becomes possible to channel that frustration into solutions. To say "my students failed me" is no doubt comforting, as it relieves us of agency, even of responsibility. It certainly does not create the anxiety of saying "I failed my students." Nor does it offer any motivation to change a single thing we do.

Perhaps I sound naive or even Pollyanna-ish here. To be sure, I have no shortage of respect and fondness for my students. I teach many first-generation students whose road to my classroom involved a lot more personal sacrifice and hard work than did my own. But even with those whose life stories more closely approximate my relatively privileged one, I cannot deny that much of my excitement to teach stems from my quite favorable attitude toward those I teach. That said, I emphatically do not deny that students can be frustrating to work with – my point is simply that students, like teachers, are made, not born, and teachers bear some responsibility for their making. So, yes, in any given semester we might face students who are lazy, poorly prepared, overly entitled, and constantly texting. That, however, is the nature of the challenge, the *starting* point. Where we go from there is what we call teaching.

I can already hear you complain: "You have reduced teaching to a personality contest, where only the most inspiring can succeed and where education becomes 'edutainment.'"[21] The concern here is palpable: Virginia Brackett speaks for many when she confesses, "[t]he claim that students remain dependent upon an instructor's ability to create a perky, positive, optimistic environment slams like a chain mail cloak across my sagging shoulders."[22] The problem with this complaint is not only that it *itself* reduces teaching to personality, but also that it conflates inspiring students to learn with high-energy, high-production-value, multisensory, cosmic experiences. Inspiration comes in many forms, however; it does not rely on overt excitement and shrieks of joy, nor does it have to involve high levels of energy and the demonstrative enthusiasm of teachers. Interest in learning often is sparked when there is no personality involved at all: books can inspire us with flowery prose or outrageous claims, but also simply by offering explanations whose clarity alone captivate us. Choosing the right reading or, more mundanely, planning a course wisely – two things you do before the course even begins – count as "teaching as motivating." Indeed, given the range of tools at your disposal – lecturing, discussion leading, project-based learning, student-peer feedback, simulations, case studies, and so on[23] – the simple act of deciding among them often constitutes the course's defining pedagogical act.[24]

Research on motivation reinforces this point: the factors that are crucial to students' motivation (about which, more below) have little to do directly with the instructor's personality. Why would they? Being motivated to learn in a meaningful sense implies working for rewards intrinsic to one's own systems of value rather than with reference to whatever regiment of extrinsic pleasures and pains the instructor might create. Learning *for* anyone but oneself is not motivated learning, and it is certainly not learning that's likely to last much beyond the end of the student-faculty relationship.

Still, to say that the instructor's personality is not the central issue is *not* to say that what the instructor does or how she carries herself is unimportant – the instructor can do many things to maximize the odds that her students will want to learn. Students might be motivated despite what we do, or wholly *un*inspired despite our best efforts,[25] but neither outcome suggests that we should withhold whatever motivation we have to study our disciplines and to teach those disciplines to them. Studies show that students' perceptions of their instructors' enthusiasm – both about their discipline and about teaching it – play an important role in how they perceive a course.[26] Enthusiasm – in effect, the motivation to engage in inquiry – can be modeled. To do so you need not have the ability to dazzle a crowd, but simply the willingness to allow students to see that you, perhaps in some nerd-like fashion, really enjoy what you are doing. If *that* bar is too high, then perhaps teaching, *whatever that means*, is not for you – although, if you insist on doing it anyway, in Chapter Two I offer a few suggestions for faking it.

Specific Considerations

The complaint that I might be pushing theatrics gets at a larger and quite understandable concern: motivating people to teach themselves is a difficult, at times daunting, task. There is a vast literature on the topic, and so I can only hope to skim across its surface,[27] but let me now, in concluding this chapter, do just that. Let's begin with a list of the more commonly cited factors that increase student motivation. All things being equal, students are more motivated to learn when they:

a. see the relevance of the subject matter;
b. are working toward high standards (and perceive their instructors to have high expectations);
c. feel their instructors are supportive of their efforts to learn;

d. find the feedback they get to be encouraging and not harshly critical;

e. do not get overly anxious about their performance on tests and assignments;

f. have confidence that they can do the work;

g. feel ownership of their learning;

h. learn actively;

i. have an interest in mastering the material, rather than in performing well on tests; and

j. see their learning as having intrinsic value.

The important thing to note about this list of student activities and perspectives is that every item on it suggests a corresponding teaching strategy – an action on the instructor's part that works toward a learning environment conducive to these activities and perspectives. Hence, to work down the list, instructors can promote student motivation when they:

a. demonstrate the relevance of the subject matter;

b. set high standards and have high expectations of student success;

c. create a safe and supportive learning environment;

d. provide students with feedback that encourages them to continue working and is not harshly critical of what they have done;

e. are aware of, and work to minimize, student anxiety over tests and assignments;

f. work to give students confidence to do what is required of them and to make the adjustments suggested in assessments of their work;

g. show students that they have control over their learning;

h. employ active learning techniques; and

i. emphasize what makes the class material worth learning.

In the appendix to this chapter, I provide several concrete examples of these activities. For now, note two aspects of this list. First, it offers clear evidence of my primary point that teaching is not about transfer of knowledge: every one of these activities can be done in the absence of any direct student acquisition of knowledge – we might, in doing any of them, meet no substantive objective for a course, no learning outcome. To be sure, many of the activities quite possibly could *involve* knowledge acquisition (in the feedback we provide, for instance), but we can think of such acquisition as a fortunate and unintended ancillary benefit. So the activity itself was teaching (or so I am arguing), even though it brought to the student no new store of knowledge. Should this decoupling of teaching and knowledge acquisition worry us?[28]

No, it should not – not if we consider the second noteworthy aspect of the list: the fact that I omitted an instructor action corresponding to the final student item, "see their learning as having intrinsic value." I did so because, in its own way, every item on the second list works toward this end. Indeed, this item is, as it were, the *summum bonum* of the list: the item toward which all the others aim. At the heart of motivation theory is the ideal that students must come to see learning as important to *their* ends and purposes, not (just) those of their teachers, parents, or peers.[29] Intrinsic motivation might not in every instance be stronger than extrinsic motivation – bodily threats would probably keep the worst of students on task – but it has a better chance of resulting in learning that is deeper and longer. The reason is simple: students driven by their own ends and purposes will learn from the best teachers of all: themselves.[30] They still might need guides in that learning; they might even need the occasional extrinsic motivation.[31] What they need most, however, are reasons to accept this most basic fact about education. For that, and for that alone, there are teachers.

A Final Thought

Conceived as a craft, teaching is not on the opposite side of the coin from learning – there is no equivalence between them. We understand that fact when attempts are made to implicate teaching in all learning. In such cases we rightly counterargue that much of what is learned comes in the absence of any teaching – unless, of course, we hold to a somewhat overly broad meaning of the word "teach," as in "the lightning bolt that hit me taught me about the power of nature."[32] The equivalence is just as false in the other direction. Yes, we teach so that students might learn, but that does not mean – as it is erroneously taken to mean – that our teaching causes the learning – or worse, that teachers are the creators of learning. Nothing could be further from the truth. When done well, teaching *leads* to learning, but real learning occurs only when it is something students do for *themselves*. To put it in scientific terms, students are far better off firing their own neurons.

Hence, the idea, espoused all too frequently by faculty developers, that "teaching is all about learning" is a paradox. We think the statement puts the emphasis on what *students* are doing; in truth, it serves only to inflate the role *instructors* play in the process. When we limit the scope of teaching to motivating students, we dissolve the teaching/learning equivalence, and put an end to this pedagogical delusion. As I argued above, we do so by putting an intermediary step, – a temporal buffer, as it were – between teaching and learning: we teach (by motivating) ➔ *the students get excited* ➔ they learn (by teaching themselves). Note that, when the real learning occurs, instructors might be nowhere in sight.

Perhaps this understanding of teaching requires a dose of modesty – in the sense of accepting that we don't actually do all we suppose we do. When learning happens, then, we should not be in such a hurry to steal more credit than we deserve. I hasten to add, however, that this view of teaching hardly signals a diminished status for the craft. To the contrary, I can think of no greater achievement than having created the conditions under which students take responsibility for their own education. In achieving that end, teachers don't create *learning*. They create *learners*.[33]

Appendix:
Motivating Students to Learn

The suggestions below are meant only as a *beginning*. They are in no way comprehensive. Note as you look through them that many could be under more than one heading (as, in fact, many of them *are*).

1. Demonstrate the relevance of the subject matter.
   a. When teaching abstract concepts, start with concrete examples; in fact, it is best to *reverse* the common order used to explain a concept. Here is the common order:
      i. write the concept (cult, habeas corpus, metaphysics, species, standard deviation, prime number, calorie) on the board;
      ii. give a glossary-type definition;
      iii. explain that definition;
      iv. provide examples.

   Note that every step is an effort to remedy the confusion created by the previous one: the definition seeks to capture the word, the explanation seeks to clarify the definition, and the examples seek to concretize the explanation. Instead of each step preparing students for the next one, each is reduced to doing damage control for the preceding one. Putting aside the conceptual difficulty, we need to think about what the students experience with this order; it is not until the final step that they actually have a sense of what the concept means in the world with which they're familiar. Finally, they have a motivation to learn – if, that is, they are still listening. By reversing the order, we give students the motivation to learn at the *beginning*.[34]

  b. Where appropriate, employ case studies and "problem-based learning."
  c. Challenge students to find commonplace examples of the subject you're teaching.
  d. Encourage students to stop you at *any* point in the class and ask, "Why does this matter?"

2. Set high standards and have high expectations of student success.
  a. Don't accept late papers without a penalty.
  b. Where appropriate, make it clear that you expect students to attend class.
  c. Make it clear that you expect students to arrive on time.
  d. Provide feedback on students' work (not just a grade – see 4); make sure the feedback is timely, since timeliness is not only helpful to the students, it also models high standards.
  e. Have students draw up a contract for the course (see 7c for more details).

3. Create a safe and supportive learning environment.[35]
  a. Flag insensitive remarks and discuss why they are not permissible in the classroom.
  b. Encourage students to share with you any fears or anxieties they might have.
  c. Use weak student remarks to your advantage:
    i. think of such a remark as an unreflective thought that needs to be given voice if the more considered ideas to which the class aims are to make sense;
    ii. as such a remark often reveals a deep confusion that other students have, consider that the student has done you a favor and thank him or her for allowing you to clarify the point;
    iii. blame all student errors on yourself – you might not deserve all of the blame, but take it anyway.
    iv. Bottom line: student errors are not opportunities to flex your intellect and put them in their place! Nothing creates more tension (for everyone) in a classroom.

4. Give students feedback that encourages them to continue working and is not harshly critical.
   a. Emphasize what they have done well.
   b. Present problem areas as places improve.
   c. Don't coddle. The idea is to tap into the feedback mechanism that is most likely to motivate further learning.
   d. The more prompt the feedback, the better; if grading an assignment takes twelve hours, two six-hour days is far better from the students' perspective than six two-hour days.[36]

5. Be aware of, and work to minimize, students' anxiety over tests and assignments.
   a. Give low-stakes assignments and tests; five assignments or tests worth 20 percent each is preferable to two worth 50 percent each.
   b. Where possible, allow students to redo assignments and retake tests.

6. Work to give students the confidence they can do what you ask of them, and that they can make the adjustments you ask for in your assessment of their work.
   a. Refrain from overly onerous, confidence-crushing assignments.
   b. Offer opportunities for students to revise their work.
   c. If grades for a particular assignment or test are generally low, be open to accepting responsibility. In this regard you might:
      i. offer a retake; or
      ii. scale grades, although there are potential hazards here – see 9c.

7. Show students that they have control over their learning.
   a. Allow student input on assignments; offer a wide choice of essay topics, for instance, and encourage students to add their own topics.
   b. Offer a choice of assessment schemes – for example, two papers and one test or two tests and one paper.
   c. Have students draw up a course contract that might involve rules surrounding civility (such as cell phone use), as well as policies on late assignments and academic dishonesty. Make sure the

contract includes *your* obligations to the students (showing up on time, being prepared, and so on). Students should sign and submit the contract.

d. Emphasize that you don't give grades; students *receive* them.

e. Take time to explain your pedagogical decisions: what is behind your particular assignments and methods of assessment? why do you have a late policy? Give students the chance to discuss your reasons, and be open to incorporating their changes.

f. If possible, avail yourself of mid-semester feedback – many teaching centers will send staff to speak with your students at that time. In discussing the results with your students, let them know their views matter (as they do: you will get helpful information to use in the latter half of the course).

8. Employ active learning techniques. At the most basic level, active learning involves any pedagogical strategy that *actively* engages students in their learning. It's at the opposite end of the spectrum from a passive strategy such as lecturing. The most common forms of active learning, known as collaborative or cooperative learning, involve students working on assignments in groups. Problem-based learning – where students work on concrete problems designed to illustrate concepts and ideas – is also active, and can also involve group work. There is a voluminous literature on active learning; the best place to start is at your campus teaching center. Standard teaching texts also provide good primers.[37] Meanwhile, think about the following:

a. Interject an active moment into any class simply by asking students questions or by eliciting their responses to things you have said.

b. Go one step further by having students initially answer your questions in small groups and then report their discussions to the class.

c. Form questions that involve higher levels of learning, such as applying knowledge to unfamiliar contexts, evaluating and critically assessing theories and arguments, and even creating new theories.

  d. Allow students to explain complex material to one another – they can often do it better than we can – they speak the same language and are often more in touch with the conceptual difficulties involved than we are.
  e. Set short, in-class writing assignments that can help students express the ideas they have picked up from the class, even if what they express is how little they understood.

9. Emphasize what makes the class material worth learning.
  a. Allow and encourage students to revise their work, thereby promoting mastery of the material, rather than simply the quest for high grades.
  b. Give students feedback on assignments first, and only then, after a delay of some days, give them a grade.
  c. Avoid norm-reference grading; students should know they are being graded on the basis of their mastery of the material, not on how they compare with their peers.
  d. Show your *own* enthusiasm for the material. This is vital!

Teaching Personas

For reasons I will get to, I begin this chapter with a few confessions.

First, I have had students in the past whom I really disliked. I am not talking about being annoyed with or frustrated by them. I mean I *really* did not like them, and not just as students, but as people. If perhaps you think that, as a professor who sees individual students only for two and a half hours a week and then only in a room with many other students, I couldn't possibly have had enough exposure to *know* them, let alone dislike them, you might be right: my judgment might have been purely superficial, but I stand by it – call it intuition. These students darkened my day and, like cats who gravitate maliciously toward people who do not like them, these students seemed to revel in showing up religiously at my office hours and droning on endlessly about their difficulties with interpreting Rousseau, or their problems with the course, or with preparing for tests, or … well … who can keep track? I tend to zone out.

Second, if there's one word I cannot bear to hear uttered, it's "rubric" – meaning those little matrices that instructors share with students that indicate to them, and to the instructor, how their work is to be assessed. As soon as someone in an educational workshop even hints at rubrics, I feel an overwhelming desire to hit the snooze button, not because I'm tired, but because sleep is preferable to violence, which is the other overriding temptation. To my mind, rubrics are the distorting distillation of any and all kernels of wisdom I want my students to grasp, often presented in a manner that makes sense only to the person who created them (if that). If an assignment can be reduced to a set of boxes for my checking, it hardly seems worth my trouble to read it. The best assignments I can give are those that push students in a direction I can only guess at. And isn't the goal of education to have *students* come to see the components of good work, or should I really just tell them what they are?

Third, I once put a fly in a microwave oven. Actually, that's not completely accurate: the oven door was open, and the fly flew in of his own volition – if flies can be said to have volition. I saw the opening and, being a resourceful type, I closed it. Then came the debate: what to do? By that I don't mean defrost versus reheat; I mean, do I release the fly or indulge my curiosity? Weighing heavily in the equation was the knowledge that, once he was released, I would likely smash him with a fly swatter; that is, in fact, what I had been trying to do until he flew into the oven. He thought he could hide there. He was wrong. In the end I went with the "Dinner" setting.

So, there you have it. I don't love all of my students, I can't abide by a certain quite standard pedagogical practice, and, just for good measure, I might be a severely sadistic person, precisely the type who should not be left alone with impressionable young people. In making these confessions, I have gone some way toward laying bare my pedagogical – and overall – soul. Yet, contrary to what some might say about the powers of confession, having confessed really has not made me feel any better. I admit them only to expose myself – to induce that sense of vulnerability that comes with opening a closet door and forcibly removing for display all manner of skeletons.

The closet, however, is just the extreme. It is that part of teaching about which the teacher is actively embarrassed and/or ashamed. Another room also provokes a fair bit of anxiety – one that exists outside the realm of metaphor: the classroom. What happens there, far from the prying eyes of colleagues, is a sound indication of who we are as educators. It is the inner sanctum of our teaching selves. To let someone into this room is to invite an intimacy with which only the most self-confident could, without a hint of pathology, be comfortable.

When, as a faculty developer, I suggested to colleagues that I would have a better sense of what was going on with their teaching if I could observe their class, the response was often as if I had asked, "Mind if I observe you and your partner having sex?" People would invariably hesitate, as their visceral reply – "are you [expletive deleted] kidding me?" – would only slowly give way to reflection on the possible merits of such a visit. The fear, I have come to see, is not just about performing under the eyes of a colleague. It goes deeper than the prospect of being caught making an exaggerated or even false academic statement. (We make those daily around the water cooler anyway.) How we behave, what we do, and how we interact in the classroom all go to the heart of who we are as educators. I say this to underscore what an honor and privilege it was to spend time in other people's classrooms. It was also fascinating. While the students (and I) were experiencing the classroom environment their instructor had created, I also found myself experiencing the person behind it. In the process, I often came to see people whom I had known previously (but only outside the classroom) in a completely different light. It was as if my colleagues had literally disappeared, replaced by what I came to think of as a "teaching persona."

It took me a while to notice this phenomenon. For a long time I thought that, in observing instructors, I was seeing two elements of the classroom experience: the techniques the instructor was employing (what he or she was *doing*) and the learning environment (everything from the interpersonal communication to the "vibe" in the room). The first hint that I was also observing something else came in the really boring classes. Truth be told, the sight of hopelessly bored students has always intrigued me, as it often raises a question – "What is this instructor doing that is so damn dull?" – that is itself far from damn dull. It can be riveting to see how an otherwise engaging, articulate colleague can, when placed in front of fifteen or thirty or one hundred students, quickly dissemble into a tedious, babbling bore. Slowly, I began to think not just about the techniques and the environment, but about the person employing the techniques and – with the students – creating the environment. Let me be clear: I am not talking about the colleague who asked me to come to his or her class. I'm talking about who that colleague became – the persona he or she took on – upon entering the classroom.

It was in looking back over the myriad reports I wrote for the colleagues whose classes I had observed that the existence of a teaching persona finally sunk in. There, between the comments on which techniques were working, which were not, and what ones they might consider introducing, were remarks not just about what they *did*, but about who, in the classroom, they *were*. This realization led me to ask about the role of this persona in determining the effectiveness of the classroom. In one sense, it is an obvious consideration, as an instructor's way of being in the classroom cannot help but affect crucial variables of student learning. In another sense, however, the thought is somewhat heretical, as it comes dangerously close to saying that good teachers are born, not made, or that "good teaching is all about entertainment and personality."[1] Education specialists usually point out the evils of this idea in discussing techniques that anyone can employ – in contrast to the instructor's personality, which is thought of as something one just has and that, as a result, cannot, at least consciously, be developed. As a general bit of advice, emphasizing techniques – or, to use the title of Ken Bain's excellent book, "what the best college teachers *do*"[2] – makes sense, and Bain's book provides an excellent overview of the practices that consistently crop up among successful teachers. Quick fixes can be quite helpful, and, well, they're quick – always a virtue given the harried pace of university teaching.

That said, we ought to be cautious about divorcing the doing from the doer, as there is quite plainly a relationship between the two. Techniques are, as it were, the external manifestations of the person employing them. Think, for instance, of the following icebreaking exercise for a first day of class: the instructor asks students to tell the class their names, majors, where they're from, and, finally, what animal they would be if they were to be reincarnated. Now ask yourself two questions: First, do you know someone (yourself, perhaps) whom you could imagine employing this technique? Second, do you know someone (again yourself, perhaps) who would rather die – perhaps to come back as one of those animals – than suffer through the ensuing discussion? (I personally fit the latter description.) That you can probably answer both questions with only brief reflection on your colleagues indicates that you get my point: pedagogical techniques are personal; whether or not they are employed – and employed effectively – depends on how well they match the employer. In this sense, it is clearly not the case that anyone can (successfully) adopt any technique.[3]

This observation complements, rather than undermines, discussions of techniques and practices. At a minimum, the importance of those techniques and practices has not been lost. We can see, in fact, that much of what makes a given teaching persona educationally sound (or not) is precisely that it so naturally lends itself (or not) to certain techniques and practices. A down-to-earth persona might be successful because it leads to a continual search for ways to relate a course's subject matter to people from different generations and with different cognitive levels. Those with a friendly persona naturally will employ strategies designed to put students at ease. In both cases, success stems from what the instructor *does*; I am merely suggesting that that fact cannot be seen in isolation from who she *is*.

Or, at least, who she is *in the classroom*. Think back to those colleagues whom you could see readily adopting the icebreaking exercise. In truth, we can only infer the use of such an exercise from what we know of the colleagues we see in the hallways or at lunch. And yet the personality that decides on the technique is not necessarily that of those same people. What we do not know, unless we have set foot inside that inner sanctum, is what actually happens to our colleagues when they enter the classroom and shut – bolt, even – the door behind them. We know our colleagues; we do not, however, know their teaching personas. To be sure, who the instructor becomes in a classroom is part of who he or she is as a person. But it is surprising how often people speak differently, listen differently, and move differently, when teaching. One of the most spellbinding and engaging lecturers I have ever observed was also one of the most socially awkward individuals I have ever met. To see him in front of a class was to want to be in his presence indefinitely. To see and be around him in person was to want to be somewhere else. Although extreme, the duality he exhibited was unremarkable: not to be transformed by the experience of engaging ten, fifty, or one hundred students speaks either of a remarkable personality or, more likely, a remarkably ineffectual educator.

Now let's change the voice from passive to active: most people are certainly transformed by the experience of teaching, but to what extent can they consciously and actively bring about that transformation themselves? Is it possible to acquire a teaching persona intentionally? Certainly, we all have basic skills in this regard. Note, for a start, how readily and frequently we all adopt alter egos. We continually adapt our behavior according to context, and in some adaptations we might feel less true to ourselves than in others. In our professional lives, where we frequently have to conform to mandates not of our own making, the need to adapt (to "code switch") is especially pressing. Our speech, for instance, varies depending on whom we are with; so, too, does the substance of what we say. Have we become different people? I doubt it. Perhaps it makes more sense to say these are different moments of who we are – moments that in total *make up* who we are.

Now consider that, as educators, we often shield our personalities from our classes. When it comes to discussing one's partners, parents, children, friends, and so on, there is a wide variety of comfort levels.

Some instructors discuss the people in their lives because they feel it humanizes them. Others – I include myself – don't want to be humanized if by that word we mean that the students become familiar with the vital details of our actual, private lives. Whatever the comfort level, the common response to it involves the creation of a teaching persona. Mine not only has no family, it has no hobbies, favorite books, or movies, no special food or drinks – although, to be sure, some of it slips out. I am not attempting to project a persona devoid of character or personality; I am simply sending a message that the person students see in the classroom is a *teacher*, one constructed solely for their learning experience. My teaching persona is not a full human being: when aspects of my personal life have bearing on what is going on in my classroom, my persona can take them on, but otherwise, I am to my students a teacher, not a father, a husband, a son, or a seven-to-fourteen-drinks-a-week kind of guy. I am not a friend to other people and, as a result of keeping so many personal details out of my persona, I will not be a friend of theirs – at least until they drop the student personas and become alumni.

What I am, however, is a teacher with a personality. It is just that that personality is not constructed around the narrative that constitutes my life. This statement in no way means that I leave outside the classroom convictions and opinions that are relevant inside it. As I said, I am not trying to be *devoid* of personality – that would be an unfortunate mistake, one that Kenneth Eble has suggested might, like so many problems with university teaching, stem from the pathologies of graduate training: "Beginning teachers concerned with the proper role of personality in teaching may have to overcome some of their graduate school conditioning. The insistence upon objectivity in most scholarly pursuits seems to rule out personal opinion and expression, and graduate study may have a way of subduing personality itself."[4] Whether or not we can blame graduate school for the effort to subdue personality, we can agree that the effort reveals a fundamental misconception about the nature of teaching. To jump from claiming that an instructor should, upon entering a classroom, leave his or her religious or political views at the door to arguing that an instructor should – or could – leave behind his or her entire psyche is to jump from a proposal that is reasonable in many circumstances to one that is foolish in all of them.

So, we quite naturally create a teaching persona, and that persona has (and should have) varying degrees of *us* in it.[5] In some cases the process might be relatively unconscious; in others, though, it might involve some amount of training to be a certain way, training that, at least initially, might border on acting. We might think here of what Aristotle referred to as "habituation" – the lifelong process whereby individuals become the moral beings they are.[6] In his mind, practical virtues like generosity and courage cannot be taught in the way that math and science are taught; to acquire them, one must live and experience them. If a person is courageous, it is because she has, through her actions and those of the people around her, come to experience and understand firsthand the vices of foolhardiness and cowardice. Moreover – and here is where the comparison to teaching comes in – laws can train us to be virtuous by promoting a way of being and acting in the world that, over time, we come to own. The key is that we come to own it. A good example is ordinances against littering. When they were first introduced, people might have refrained from littering because of the sanctions imposed by the ordinances. Over time, however, the norm of not littering became accepted internally, with the result that now many of us do not litter even when no one is looking – or if we do, we feel guilty about it.

Developing a teaching persona is a similar process: if we play the part long enough, the part becomes effortless. Personally, I like and use profanity, but I realized early in my teaching career that, to the extent profanity makes some people uncomfortable, it was best to avoid it in the classroom. Training myself to find appropriate alternative words was a conscious effort at first, but it has long since become an unnoticed transition when I walk from my office to the classroom. Some might describe my effort as the adoption of a technique, but I suggest that more is going on: that I am not a swearer employing a foreign language; in the classroom, I am that very foreigner.[7]

I once got a call from a creative writing instructor who was having great problems in the classroom. His students were not motivated, and their work showed it. He was exceedingly frustrated with this state of affairs, and, he realized, his frustrations were showing. "I can't help it!" he said, speaking of his classroom outbursts of impatience. "They write crap and expect me to find something good to say about it! Who, with an ounce of artistic integrity, could suffer such ineptitude? What can I say? I'm a writer; bad writing offends me deeply."

In response I told him that I thought he was wrong. "You are *not* a writer," I said. Mildly shocked – thinking perhaps I'd read his work – he asked what the hell I meant. "From 1:00 to 2:15 on Tuesdays and Thursdays you are not a writer, you are a *teacher* of writing. The two people are related, but are in many ways as different as any two people could be. A writer writes. A teacher of writing creates a space where others can learn to write. You came to me not because you were having trouble as a writer, but because you were having trouble as a teacher of writing, and so perhaps you might think of yourself as that person. Only then can you start doing the things that person does."[8]

"OK," he replied, looking somewhat relieved, "but what, *concretely*, do you mean?"

"Well, if someone reads their piece of crap in your class, the first questions you should ask yourself are: what should a teacher of writing do? followed quickly by how can I help this student learn from this aforementioned piece of crap? The first question puts you in a frame of mind, one from which the second should arise. Acting on those questions rules out doing things a writer or a literary critic might do, and focuses instead on figuring out which elements of the crap to focus on so that the student has the intellectual energy and confidence to learn from it. A writer might rejoice or wince in the face of another's turgid prose, but a teacher of writing has to take responsibility for it. As this student's teacher, you need to entertain the notion that *you* did this to him: his piece of crap is *your* piece of crap. It might be inaccurate to say that, but doing so will begin to move you from one persona to another. Because you're responsible for the writing, you have to fix it. If you can't do that, you – the *teaching* you – fail. At that point the only question you need ask is how closely the success or failure of that persona is tied to the emotional well-being and self-esteem of the person behind it." (This, anyway, is the gist of what was, I'm sure, a far less articulately offered observation.)

My final bit of advice was that, each day, as he approached the classroom door, he stop and reflect for a moment on who he was about to become: "I am a *teacher* of writing, not a writer." In truth, he was not becoming someone he was not; he was simply adopting an attitude or perspective. In his case, however, I felt it would be healthy if he at least perceived there to be some ontological distance between the person in whom his self-esteem was invested and a "mere" teacher. Only then, with some success in the classroom, might he consider dropping the modifier "mere." Only then, in other words, might he begin to collapse the distance and think of himself not just as a writer, but also as a teacher.

The general idea here is that it might be easier and more effective to think about the pedagogically sound response to a particular classroom situation – such as a dumb question – not as a *technique*, but as something that grows from a *way of being*. Being somebody is a more profound task than doing something, but precisely because it is more profound, it might just be easier to stick with. Technique requires memory – in particular, the ability to recall a way of handling a situation in the very heat of it: what was I supposed to do when the bizarre nature of a student's question brought an engaging discussion to a screeching halt? In contrast, if we can stay in character, a way of handling any situation will grow spontaneously out of that character, rather than from the situations themselves. For instance, it is easier to listen actively to your students if you *are* in fact – or are *being* – a listener.

In a certain sense, I am suggesting that we learn to teach in the same manner that we hope our students come to learn: by having the knowledge somehow arise from within. The ideal is in contrast to what Paolo Freire referred to (quite critically) as the "banking model" of education – one in which instructors pour knowledge into their students, *telling* them, say, what the quadratic equation is or what the causes of the Crimean War were.[9] We can, in learning to teach, have someone (or some book) tell us about the myriad techniques to employ in myriad situations, but doing so can sometimes ensure only that the techniques are remembered right up until the situations actually occur. By contrast, if we also learn to *be* a certain way, the techniques we need have a way of finding us.

Parker Palmer captures something close to this idea when he says that "good teaching cannot be reduced to technique; good teaching comes from the identity and integrity of the teacher … In every class I teach, my ability to connect with my students, and to connect them with the subject, depends less on the methods I use than on the degree to which I know and trust my selfhood – and am willing to make it available and vulnerable in the service of learning."[10] Where I might differ with Palmer is with regard to the connection between the persona and the person. Palmer actually makes no distinction here; in fact, he puts his very selfhood into the classroom and, although I am not exactly clear what "selfhood" is – it sounds a bit too new-age for me – I am pretty sure it gets about as close as possible to the person. What I am suggesting, however, is that, while our teaching persona is a part of who we are – it could hardly be otherwise – it might be a more distant relative than we commonly acknowledge. In fact, for some, a successful teaching persona might be more akin to a heuristic for educational success than an extension of one's natural impulses.

The general point on which Palmer and I agree, however, is one that many in education seem reluctant to acknowledge – namely, that our classroom personality affects the learning environment we help to create.[11] Think, after all, what it would mean for an instructor to be *devoid* of personality. It's not easy. Can we envision anything that an instructor does that would *not* reveal something about her psychological state? More to the point, would we want to eliminate techniques that obviously *do* reveal such a state? Personal anecdotes personalize discourse, and in so doing pique the interest of anyone listening – and even those who initially are not. It is a technique, but surely one that exudes personality – indeed, it *depends* upon the expression of personality. The simple choice about what aspect of one's life to reveal says something, irrespective of how much the actual story reveals. In short, to say that an instructor's personality is not part of what happens in the classroom is never to have set foot in a classroom, and it is certainly not to recognize what makes many teaching personas work well.

In thinking about teaching personas, I keep coming back to the question: how distinct from the underlying person can they be? Clearly the greater the distance between the person and the persona, the greater the degree of difficulty and the lower the degree of plausibility. Beyond a certain point, the persona will cease to provide effective cover. But *what is* that point? I have no good answer, but I would argue that the academic literature, to the extent that it addresses matters even close to the issue,[12] might be overly pessimistic about our plasticity. In his discussion of how people develop teaching *styles* – which are somewhat different than personas – Grasha speaks of a rigorous psychological journey involving a fairly thorough self-examination, not just of existing styles, but of whatever "psychological factors within us ... facilitate and hinder our ability to vary our styles."[13] For Grasha, teaching style "represents those enduring personal qualities and behaviors that appear in how we conduct our classes." In other words, how we teach is bound tightly to who we *are*, or, as Eble puts it, "Style [is] 'what one is.'"[14] With this thought in mind, Grasha concludes that one's style "is not something that is put on for the occasion. Otherwise, it becomes a superficial covering, mask, or a collection of interesting mannerisms that are used to create an impression."[15]

I am suggesting precisely that a persona *can* be put on for the occasion; that it can be less what one is than what one projects. Again, I don't know what limits there might be to the person/persona gulf, but I do think there will be times when the persona might be nothing more than "a collection of interesting mannerisms that are used to create an impression," and that these times might persist indefinitely. But that's not necessarily a problem. Although it is true that a pronounced distance between the persona and its owner is not an optimal state of affairs, in some instances it might be preferable to the alternative – that is, to being who we really are.

Consider a professor – perhaps a very burned-out professor – who has lost all enthusiasm for the subject matter she is teaching. What should she do? How should she approach the class material? My advice would be to fake it. If you cannot actually be enthusiastic, try to put yourself in the mindset of someone who *is*, and from there ask the relevant question about technique: what would an enthusiastic person do right about now? Anyone who is genuinely shocked to hear this advice should consider the alternative: should faculty really voice the low opinion they might have of the subject they are perhaps being forced to teach? Which makes more pedagogical sense: strategic disingenuousness (acting) or shoot-yourself-in-the-foot honesty? To the extent that the determinant of student learning is often the perception students have of such matters, the professor's true underlying mental state would be largely irrelevant. All that would matter is that the persona projects various traits to which students respond positively. It would certainly be best if instructors always respected all their students and cared about their learning. But for those who, in their true state, can muster neither sentiment – and for whom neither retirement nor a career in aeronautics is an option – a persona oozing with respect and care is a plausible alternative.

Let me go one step further and suggest that such acting is not really disingenuousness at all. In forcing a conceptual wedge between the person and the persona, we can think of them as different people, even if in fact they are different moments in the same life. As such, what is true of one need not be true of the other. If one lacks certain virtues, the other might possess them. Admittedly, it is a stretch to say that the persona *has* a virtue that the person behind it does not, but when we shift the focus from virtues we lack to baggage we carry, the scenario is more plausible. Here we ask our persona not to acquire dispositions we *do* not have, but rather to shed those we *should* not have. What made my dislike of the occasional student unproblematic is that, in truth, it was *I*, not my teaching persona, who disliked him. Viewed through the lens of a persona, my personal unsavory view became, from a pedagogical standpoint, irrelevant. As I did not have to see any one student for more than a few hours a week, it was not difficult to adopt a persona that felt none of my personal malice and that was therefore capable of fostering the learning of a student whose neck I would have wrung at the drop of a hat.

To be sure, a baggage-free persona is a critical standard, not an attainable goal. But it is something always to keep in mind, even if we must of necessity always have a few packed bags closely at hand in our dealings with those around us. But how, precisely, do we keep such a persona in mind? The simplest strategy, as I have suggested, is to approach the educational situations we confront with the question: How would someone without the baggage we have handle this situation? What, in other words, would that persona do? The heavier the baggage, the more important the thought experiment becomes. An extreme example comes from a conversation I had with a friend about his parents' impending holiday visit. He is gay, and his parents have accepted his sexuality, as he put it, "as one accepts gravity ... It's a reality that they can't deny, but they don't embrace it." He explained that his Christmas decorations included several figurines of naked men and other overtly gay iconography. When I asked about this plan to antagonize his parents, he responded by saying that they had thrown Christianity and heterosexuality in his face all his life; now it was his turn. More important, he wanted them to know who he was. In response I asked him – as he is a superb teacher – whether he thought this technique was pedagogically sound. If he wanted his parents to learn something, as opposed to merely antagonizing them, did he think this technique – making them angry and defensive – would work? He confessed that perhaps it would not, at which point the conversation turned to a discussion of the relative merits of antagonizing versus educating. (I do not intend to diminish the pleasures of the former.)

I left the conversation thinking to myself that this would be the gold standard for persona adoption: truly gifted teaching would involve the ability to teach one's parents ... *anything*. For most of us there is no other relationship so wrought with baggage, and that baggage often undermines our ability to explain to parents the values we have come to hold and, more generally, the person we have become. Doing so successfully would involve taking many deep breaths and putting aside whatever "issues" such conversations raise. It would, in other words, involve adopting the ultimate teaching persona, one that manages to purge our deepest and sometimes darkest inner selves. (As I discovered in my disastrous attempts to teach my children to drive, the parallel ideal of teaching one's children might be equally good.)

What the ideal highlights is that to get inside someone else's head – which we must do if we are to figure out how to help them learn – we first must get inside our own. Despite my dislike for the occasional student – and, to be clear, it's an exceedingly rare event – I have always understood that my job was to teach them. In so doing I tried to figure out what caused me to feel such antipathy, and then developed a persona that not only ignored those feelings, but was genuinely enthused by seeing the student learn. To provide some context: arrogance and a lack of curiosity are two things that get on my nerves. In the world outside the classroom, I avoid people who exhibit an abundance of either. Among students, unfortunately, these two traits are hardly rare; in fact, they often seem to run hand in hand. So, what to do? The first step is fairly basic: realize that the requirements of friendship and those of a healthy teacher/student relationship have no necessary connection to each other. The "I" who enjoys the company of friends is not the same "I" who works with students. The first looks for likability in those around him; the second seeks, for lack of a better word, teachability. The first has no time for arrogance or incuriousness; the second relishes encounters with both. And why not? To infuse arrogance with humility or doubt and incuriousness with awe is to achieve an incomparable measure of success, one that lies well beyond the grasp of the first "I." So why would the first "I" not happily hand the reins of a course over to the second? (One might suggest that my real self could take a lesson from my persona and work, in my day-to-day life, to help the arrogant and lazy become better people. My reply is that life is too short for such mission-ary endeavors, and besides, refusing to tolerate certain types of people has its own rewards.)

In a sense, then, my teaching persona is there to remind me that my immediate objective is to teach, not – more vitally – to put arro-gance and incuriousness in their place. In another sense, "remind" is not exactly right: the idea is that, by staying in character, I will need no reminding because my persona is the one who is teaching. Certain duties of teaching do not always come naturally to me; at such times, rather than stretch my capacities to the limit, I simply employ someone better suited to the task. Again, adopting the persona involves a certain discipline of its own, but the resultant harmony between the doer and the deed is, in the end, a far easier and less stressful way to approach the limits of my own personality.

So I stand by my dislike of a few students, just as I do my disdain for rubrics. At least I don't feel the need to deny, work through or otherwise correct either. The point, after all, is to render such thoughts superflu-ous, especially on days when my less savory impulses threaten to get the best of me.

At this point, you might object that this discussion of personas is out of place in a book on teaching as a craft. Is it really a craft when the craftsperson is reduced to creating an alter ego just to get through the day? Doesn't craftwork go to the heart of the person doing it – not, by extension, to some separable persona? My response to such questions is the same: a craft involves more than just adopting the techniques of its practitioners. One must not merely "put on a face," but find a part of oneself that feels genuine.[16] Craftwork is a state of being, not a compendium of tasks to be completed. It is not just *doing something*; it is *being someone*. That someone – that persona – might not, in outward appearance, be exactly like the person behind it, but we should not conclude therefore that the activity is not the person's. To adopt a persona is not to divorce oneself from the craft activity; to the contrary, it is to establish a relationship with the craft that goes well beyond the mere application of techniques.

To be sure, the more distance between the person and the persona, the more the person is a *troubled* craftsperson. Note, however, that I still wish to call her a craftsperson – and I do so precisely in virtue of her having adopted a persona. In so doing, she is responding to whatever difficult personal and/or structural (economic, institutional) situation she confronts not merely by doing certain *things* ("remedial techniques for the burned out"). Her response is more deep-seated. It's rooted not in what she does but in how she approaches what she does. In saying, "if I cannot do my job, then I will conceive of it not as a job at all, but as something *more* – a calling, perhaps," she is responding to an employment problem with a craft solution. Rather than try to turn an unacceptably lousy job into a barely acceptably lousy one, she fights the dread of her situation by rejecting it *as* a job. She accepts that the dread stems precisely from its being a job. Even if such a perspective does not lead over time to a gradual narrowing of the person/persona gap – if, in other words, the alienation persists – she will, I maintain, have settled on the response that most effectively addresses the underlying problem. As I stated in the Introduction, teaching as a craft is an act of rebellion, and as with all acts of rebellion it is to be judged not simply by whether it succeeds in changing some existing practice, but also by how well it helps us to cope with that practice in the event that it remains in place.[17]

So, what makes for a good persona? In the final year of my tenure as a faculty developer, I sought out my campus's master teachers – those with a legendary reputation among students and faculty – and asked if I could observe their classes. I then embarked on a wholly unscientific study, one designed to provide only a very broad and preliminary picture of good personas. I began by simply observing and by writing down the adjectives that came to mind – words that captured the presence with which they conducted their classes. The words were much as one would expect: friendly, quirky, enthusiastic (even excited), patient, down-to-earth, clear and articulate, respectful, intellectually curious, empathetic,[18] energetic, somewhat nervous (and thus often quite peripatetic[19]), caring, listening, secure, funny,[20] commanding (in their presence). A formidable list, but I should quickly point out that no one persona had all or even most of these traits – in fact, I doubt a persona with all those traits is even psychologically possible. Many personas were not what one would describe as funny; many others were not in the slightest bit quirky. While never *unfriendly*, many had an all-business air about them that exuded not an ounce of friendliness.[21]

Still, there were a few *sine qua non*s. All personas clearly exhibited enthusiasm, both for what they taught and for the act of teaching it, albeit sometimes in a very low-key manner.[22] None was impatient, insecure (about their own grasp of the material) or disrespectful. All were down-to-earth, attentive to what their students said and asked, and all projected concern that learning was taking place. Of course, I cannot be certain that the people behind the personas were *themselves* enthusiastic, patient, secure, respectful, down-to-earth, listening, and/or caring – and, in a sense, that is precisely the point. These were the personas people projected, not, of necessity, the people themselves.

And this point raises a reasonable question: just how adoptable *are* these personas? Are some personas ill-suited to certain temperaments? To be sure, one can only adopt a persona with which one is comfortable. As I have mentioned, to be worn effectively, a persona must feel true at some level. Even where there is a fair degree of acting involved, the basic psychological state must be one that the instructor is capable of experiencing and expressing. One need not be enthusiastic about organic chemistry, but to teach it with enthusiasm requires one to be at least capable of the emotion.

Think about the example of empathy. Can anyone really just adopt an empathetic persona? And are we even talking about a persona when we discuss the ability to detect body language or energy levels? Clearly, the answer to both questions is no, and yet it is equally clear that we gain something in the simple recognition that empathetic personas are effective. Perhaps one cannot simply become empathetic or acquire certain states of awareness, but it is helpful just the same to know that successful instructors have these particular traits and abilities. With such knowledge, one without these abilities can begin to think about what compensatory strategies might achieve the success of those more fortunately endowed.

Consider the trait of being down-to-earth, a trait sometimes lacking in academics. A science professor once came to see me who was a brilliant and accomplished researcher. His classes, however, were giving him fits. His students, he explained, simply did not understand even the most basic concepts. As I often did in such cases, I asked him about those concepts to find out what sort of explanation he might offer someone who was in neither his field nor his class. As I expected from someone whose students were struggling, whatever understanding I had of the concepts before he began to speak was lost within thirty seconds. The more he spoke, the less I knew. Pressing him further, about ever simpler concepts, proved increasingly disastrous. Within minutes the modest confidence I had in my knowledge of these concepts was replaced by the despondency that comes with realizing the depth of one's ignorance.[23] His ability to relate to me – a requirement of someone attempting to relate *concepts* to me – seemed beyond hopeless. Obviously, telling him simply to *become* down-to-earth – to relate better to his students – would have been about as effective as telling a humorless person to be funny. A down-to-earth persona was not available to him.

So, what to do? My solution was to suggest that, if he couldn't relate the subject matter to his students, he should enlist the help of those who could. We are not, after all, the only instructors in the room. The single greatest purpose in bringing students together in one place at one time is not to avoid having to give thirty lectures to thirty audiences of one; it is to provide a *social* learning experience that is unavailable to any single student.[24] To create that experience, we need to keep in mind that our classrooms are filled with potential co-conspirators. "*Your students!*" I implored him. "Use *them* to explain these concepts. Because there are many of them, you can get more than one take on an explanation, and – best of all – the explanations will take a form to which they can relate ('I never thought about this before, but I think the idea is that …'), and will be delivered in a language they understand. The fact that every third word might be 'like,' in no way diminishes the accuracy or clarity of the explanation."

In a sense I was suggesting that he *subcontract* a down-to-earth persona, an out-of-body alter-ego. What this means, of course, is that the students who answer questions and discuss their thoughts with the rest of the class are actually creating their own personas and, in so doing, acting in a manner they might not otherwise. They are, in effect, trying to *teach*. If there were any greater defense of the classroom experience than that, I cannot imagine what it would be.

More vitally still, in subcontracting out this persona, the professor does not just foster the creation of numerous other personas; he also creates an entirely different sort of persona: a purely social one, one that captures the intersubjective gestalt of the class. A class in which all work to educate all is one that moves and acts in a particular way. It has its own unique character, its own persona. We could think of this as a teaching persona, but it makes more sense to call it a *learning* persona. Thought of in this way, the role of the instructor becomes one of monitoring that persona, of staying acutely attuned to how it is doing. Learning, after all, is the product not so much of the instructor, but of the environment he helps to create – an environment (or, to use Fink's language, "a significant learning experience")[25] fostered in part by activities and techniques but emphatically not reducible to them.[26]

So, although I have focused on who instructors *are* in the classroom, and others have focused on all that they *do*, my concluding thought is that who we are and what we do matter only to the extent that they result in a persona – a single *collective* essence – that is irreducible to either.

One more word about that poor fly in the microwave oven. Perhaps you thought that I should have herded him out of the oven, if only just to squash him. Or perhaps you thought that, if his death was inevitable, better to have left him in the microwave until he died of natural causes – although I'm not sure how sitting in a microwave oven qualifies as natural, even for a fly. I see the merit in both alternatives, especially if my actions are to be judged on their moral content. In that regard, the problem with my course of action, as I see it, is that it involved my taking an interest in the fly's death. Before it flew into the microwave, my only interest was in having it be nowhere near me. As is often the case with insects, its death was the most effective option, but not my primary concern. The death that results from squashing a fly is ancillary and, as callous and insensitive to arthropod life as that sounds, merely a *byproduct* of my interest, which makes my action seem morally more palatable.

Now I could defend myself by arguing that death in the name of scientific curiosity is more morally justified than death in the name of idle comfort – my fly gave himself (although, in truth, *I* gave him) to science rather than merely to assuage my aversion to itching. My interest, however, is not to get off the moral hook, but to ask whether my action, however one adjudicates it, makes a difference to my career as an educator of impressionable young people. If you have followed me thus far, you can anticipate my argument that it does not. Parents of impressionable youth can take comfort in the knowledge that the twisted mind that watched a fly die[27] is not the one that teaches their children. I do my best to keep *that* mind unsullied by the depravities which have no bearing on student learning.[28] In this particular case, I kept the depravity to myself while ceding to my persona the intellectual curiosity that gave rise to it – or perhaps that served to justify it. In other cases, similar parsing takes place. My teaching persona, for instance, has never inhaled. Whether or not *I* have is, from an educational standpoint, quite irrelevant.

Words that Teach

I write these words with some degree of dread because I know that you, the reader, can linger over any of them for as long as you like. You can stop and reflect on any claim I make or theory I propose. You can pick the whole of it apart. Had I just told you my ideas, and had I done so in a particularly persuasive manner, the gaps in my logic might have eluded you. Of course, you could also have missed the gaps as you read them, but in such cases there would always be time to go back and correct your (and thus my) error. A fundamental peace thus escapes me: at any point in the future my shortcomings could be laid bare. All things considered, the written word is the enemy of those who wish not to be kept honest.

I dwell on the negative here because my perspective is that of the writer, not the reader. Yet what worries the writer is music to the reader's ears: an idea, expressed in writing, can sink in slowly – it can fester, bother, clarify … and excite. It can, in other words, *teach*.

It is easy to forget that much of a course's learning happens outside the classroom, in the activities and assignments students complete and (with most courses) in the reading they do. I say it's easy to forget because we often use class periods to "cover" what the students were supposed to learn from their reading. So we assign reading with the idea that students will learn outside the classroom, but then we use the classroom to "teach" them what they were supposed to learn on their own. The architecture of whole courses rest on this absurdity: syllabi contain lists of assigned texts and dates for required reading, and they are never labeled, as they should be, "Readings that you *won't* do." It's a puzzling logic. We teach on a model that explicitly rejects the very assumptions with which we begin.

Am I being too cynical? I doubt it. If you assumed your students were actually learning from the reading you gave them, would you prepare a class in the same way you usually do? I suspect that if you did make this assumption, your approach would look oddly wrong – wrong because you'd worry that your students, having actually done the reading, would be bored with it. I further suspect that, in preparing your classes, you do assume at least *some* lack of learning from the reading. The problem, of course, is that your assumption is likely justified, and thus denying it would lead you to prepare a class for students whom you are not currently teaching.[1]

So, what to do? Preparing for the students we are likely to have (the ones who haven't read) often results in turning off the very students we *aspire* to have (those who *have* read and have come prepared to take their learning to the next level). Is there is a strategy that allows instructors to have it both ways – to teach to the students they aspire to have *as well as* those they *do* have? If we keep in mind my central theme – that craft teaching is about motivating students to teach themselves – there is such a strategy. The key is somehow to *complement* the reading, to offer a class that neither regurgitates it nor presupposes any great knowledge of it. An obvious and general example would be to raise issues the reading touches upon without actually referring specifically to it. If done well, the students who have completed the reading will have their understanding of it enriched; those who have not might be inspired to run from the classroom to the bookstore or library and get right at it.

Easier said than done. "Go inspire!" I say. Great, but how exactly? Elsewhere in this book, particularly in Chapter One, I have offered a few answers. What I have tried to emphasize throughout, however, is that much of teaching exists behind the scenes, in the way we devise assignments and activities, assess student work, structure whole courses – in short, in the way we create the overall learning environment. The reality of education is that most of the time we want students to spend on our course is actually spent *outside* the classroom and out of our sight, so it follows that crucial aspects of teaching come in thinking about how we want students to spend that time.

Which leads us back to reading. We want to structure class time so that students leave wanting to – *dying* to – tackle the assigned readings (either for the class they just left or for the next one – or for both). It is important, however, that the readings not undo the enthusiasm generated in class. If teaching is about generating enthusiasm for learning, our choice of readings must also contribute to that goal. The readings must help create an endless cycle in which reading leads to a desire for more reading. They must, in other words, inspire by proxy.

But can academic readings really inspire? They can, and they have. One famous inspirational incident involves Thomas Hobbes, whose intellectual life was radically altered by a chance reading of Euclid. In John Aubrey's famous seventeenth-century account,

> [Hobbes] was 40 yeares old before he looked on Geometry; which happened accidentally. Being in a Gentleman's Library, Euclid's Elements lay open, and 'twas the 47 El. Libri 1. He read the proposition. By G-, sayd he (he would now and then sweare an emphaticall Oath by way of emphasis) this is impossible! So he reads the Demonstration of it, which referred him back to such a Proposition; which proposition he read. That referred him back to another, which he also read. Et sic deinceps [and so on] that at last he was demonstratively convinced of that trueth. This made him in love with Geometry.

In my introductory lecture on Hobbes, I, perhaps like most political philosophers, always read Aubrey's account to my students. My purpose is to emphasize how indebted Hobbes's philosophical method was to the reasoning embedded in geometric proofs. At the same time, I hope my students also pick up the subtler message that, at any moment and without warning, their world might be rocked by something they see – by words on a page or, more likely in their cases, on a screen. Euclid's 47th Proposition – the Pythagorean Theorem – is only about fifty words long, and is dominated by a diagram. There is utility in its wording but not style. For Hobbes, however, it somehow "made him in love."

The history of political philosophy has at least one other famous "reading moment." The philosopher was Rousseau, and in this case the words were merely a question posted on a sign: "Has the restoration of the arts and sciences had the effect of purifying or corrupting morals?" In reading these words, Rousseau reports that "[t]he moment I had read this, I seemed to behold another world, and became a different man." As we might imagine, the event was traumatic:

> If anything ever resembled a flash of inspiration, it is the turmoil that took place within me upon reading that announcement. Suddenly I feel my spirit dazzled by a thousand brilliant insights. A host of ideas crowd in upon me all at once, troubling my mind with a force and confusion impossible to express. I feel my head spinning with a giddiness like intoxication. A violent palpitation oppresses and expands my breast. Finding it no longer possible to breathe while walking, I let myself collapse beneath one of the trees which line the avenue; there I spend half an hour in such a state of agitation that in rising I discover the front of my vest to be wet with tears I never knew I had shed.[2]

I can't say that any question I have composed has ever elicited a response of this sort – at least to my knowledge. Nor can I say for certain that the words in the Academy's question elicited this one. Rousseau is an unreliable source. And yet there was clearly something about the question that managed to pull out of him thoughts about which he might have been only inchoately aware. The question to ask is, what was that something? Both Hobbes and Rousseau were inspired, startlingly so, by words. In both cases the inspiration led to study, reflection, and the generation of theories that have had a profound impact on intellectual (if not actual) history. But how did it happen? When do words have the ability both to transfer knowledge *and* inspire further learning?

It is probably not possible to come up with a one-size-fits-all rule here, but that said, I think there might be at least one "meta-rule" for teaching words – one element that we can see throughout a wide variety of reading. And here I should be clear: I'm not referring to how one should construct a how-to manual or a text in which it is important to avoid jargon or use helpful graphics. My concern is more immediate: when do words, small numbers of them in particular, manage to spark a particular sort of thought – one that compels us to seek out more of them?

In answering, let's begin with examples that seem to work. Obvious ones come from fiction, and here I'm not thinking of prose that in some parsimonious manner manages to evoke endless and fascinating images. Hemingway's (alleged) six-word short story – "For sale, children's boots, never worn." – does precisely that, but I would not say that these words create learning in the present or future. The fiction I have in mind is more like James Joyce's introduction of Miss Devlin in the short story "A Mother," from *Dubliners*:

Miss Devlin had become Mrs. Kearney out of spite. She had been educated in a high-class convent, where she had learned French and music. As she was naturally pale and unbending in manner she made few friends at school. When she came to the age of marriage she was sent out to many houses where her playing and ivory manners were much admired. She sat amid the chilly circle of her accomplishments, waiting for some suitor to brave it and offer her a brilliant life. But the young men whom she met were ordinary and she gave them no encouragement, trying to console her romantic desires by eating a great deal of Turkish Delight in secret. However, when she drew near the limit and her friends began to loosen

their tongues about her, she silenced them by marrying Mr. Kearney, who
was a bootmaker on Ormond Quay.

The first time I read this passage, I was struck by two things. First, I
couldn't believe what a clear picture of Miss Devlin I had gotten from
such a short passage; second, I wanted more – I was immediately hooked.
Joyce's words evoke a powerful image and, I like to think, in a way that
captivates anyone who reads them. There is an arresting clarity to them
that is at the root of their ability to teach us something – ironic, given
that Joyce would go on to *Finnegans Wake*, which, whatever its virtues,
has probably done more to put an end to reading than a beginning.

Yet my sense is that clarity is not the first characteristic people might
come up with if asked to describe their reactions to these words. Because
the passage is fiction, they might remark on its beauty and then, if pushed
to elaborate, on its vivid imagery, its turn of phrase, its ability to evoke,
its parsimony. In attempting to understand beauty, however – because
we think that's what is required for an appreciation of literature – people
likely would omit virtues of a more utilitarian sort. Clarity would be one
such casualty. Whether or not clarity is a constituent of beauty is not
the point; rather, it is simply that clarity is what grabs us, what teaches
us. I don't mean here only that the writer manages to transfer, transparently and unambiguously, ideas to the reader, but that, in so doing, the
words *clarify* ideas the reader already had in mind. The words don't just
connect the reader to the writer, but also the reader to herself. "Eureka"
moments do not happen when we learn something about which we had
no prior idea; they happen because some event causes our ideas to crys-
talize in a new way.

Here's an example. A math concept that always struck me as
arbitrary – meaning conventional, rather than tied to some properties
intrinsic to mathematics – was how the plus and minus signs work out
when we multiply positive and negative numbers. Perhaps you remember:
multiply two positives together and you get a positive ($2 \times 3 = 6$); multiplying two negatives also makes a positive ($-2 \times -3 = 6$); but a negative

and a positive yield a negative $(-2 \times 3 = -6)$. "Says who?" I would think to myself. It seemed arbitrary to me. Were I ever to start a planet, it would be different, I thought. Two negatives would be *really* negative, perhaps. That's what the French and Italians do with words, after all: "Je *ne* sais *pas*"; "*Non* so *niente*." My problem, of course, was that I couldn't envision multiplying anything by a negative number. What would that mean?

One day I got an answer. I happened upon the following explanation, one that amounts essentially to a translation of numbers into words:

$3 \times 5 = 15$: getting five dollars three times is getting fifteen dollars;

$3 \times (-5) = -15$: paying a five-dollar penalty three times is a fifteen-dollar penalty;

$(-3) \times 5 = -15$: not getting five dollars three times is not getting fifteen dollars;

$(-3) \times (-5) = 15$: not paying a five-dollar penalty three times is getting fifteen dollars.[3]

The words stopped me cold. The rules I had learned *did* capture the nature of numbers. My contingency theory crumbled – and with it the specialness of my planet. No matter – I got it! Forty-some-odd words altered a lifetime of brooding – brooding that invariably put an end to whatever energy I might have devoted to thinking about multiplying positive and negative numbers. Had I been armed with this newfound understanding of why products work out the way they do, I … well to be honest, I haven't given the matter much more thought, but had I been a student in a math class, my excitement over this stroke of awareness could easily have prompted further thought, or perhaps even action: a change in major perhaps. Emboldened by confidence – what clarity delivers, after all – there's no telling how far I might have run with my new thoughts: six books stolen from the library had fifty pages each; the library is lacking three hundred pages!

Perhaps you are thinking that the real teaching was done by the ideas expressed in the words, not by the actual words themselves. But I have difficulty seeing how we won't give due credit to the words themselves: an idea I could never get my head around somehow seemed so obvious, all because it was explained in a manner that struck a chord. The medium was the message here.

Let's try another mathematical example, this one a bit more advanced. If you look up "fractal" in the dictionary, you'll get a definition like this one, from *Merriam-Webster*: "any of various extremely irregular curves or shapes for which any suitably chosen part is similar in shape to a given larger or smaller part when magnified or reduced to the same size." If that doesn't help, there is *Wikipedia*'s somewhat circular "a mathematical set that has a fractal dimension that usually exceeds its topographical dimension and may fall between the integers." At this point you might decide you can live without knowing what a fractal is. That decision would be unfortunate, for not only are fractals mathematically fascinating; the basic idea behind them is actually quite straightforward, as you will see readily from Jim Holt's description in the *New York Review of Books* of self-similarity, the defining characteristic of fractals:

> To see what self-similarity means, consider a homely example: the cauliflower. Take a head of this vegetable and observe its form – the way it is composed of florets. Pull off one of those florets. What does it look like? It looks like a little head of cauliflower, with its own subflorets. Now pull off one of those subflorets. What does *that* look like? A still tinier cauliflower. If you continue this process – and you may soon need a magnifying glass – you'll find that the smaller and smaller pieces all resemble the head you started with. The cauliflower is thus said to be self-similar. Each of its parts echoes the whole.[4]

To be fair, this comparison is *not* fair: dictionaries and online encyclopedias have a different function than do articles in popular magazines. And that's the point: if we want students to be excited readers, we need to think seriously about what we ask them to read. We do not, I hope, assign dictionaries and encyclopedias, because we understand that these resources are designed more to inform than to teach. We do assign textbooks, but these, too – though designed to teach – are often far better at informing. (They make a lot of money, too, a fact that helps explain why they inform so many people.) I would wager that textbooks account for a disproportionately high percentage of the readings regurgitated in class periods. Why? Because teachers understand that, even if students do the reading, it will not have, in my sense of the word, *taught* them much. The impulse to regurgitate just makes matters worse: class periods spent going over every point made in the textbook hardly motivate students to run home and crack open their own copy; and if they do, it will lead only to disappointment.

Having one's chord struck is a subjective thing, of course, but here is a passage that got me:

> There is so much confusion surrounding the notions of objectivity and subjectivity that I need to say a word to clarify them. In one sense, the objective/subjective distinction is about claims to knowledge. I call this the epistemic sense. A claim is said to be objective if its truth or falsity can be settled as a matter of fact independent of anybody's attitudes, feelings, or evaluations; it is subjective if it cannot. For example, the claim that Van Gogh died in France is epistemically objective. But the claim that Van Gogh was a better painter than Gauguin is, as they say, a matter of subjective opinion. It is epistemically subjective.
>
> In another sense, the objective/subjective distinction is about modes of existence. I call this the ontological sense. As entity has an objective ontology if its existence does not depend on being experienced by a human or animal subject; otherwise it is subjective. For example mountains, molecules, and tectonic plates are ontologically objective. Their existence does not depend on being experienced by anybody. But pains, tickles, and itches exist only when experienced by a human or animal subject. They are ontologically subjective.[5]

What this passage points to is that good pedagogical writing does not need to be sexy or poetic. Clarity itself is sometimes enough: understanding serves as its own source of excitement. In this example, as in the multiplication example, we see that clarity is greatly aided by the use of concrete examples that anyone can grasp. We all can see that mountains and itches exist in nature in slightly different ways. As we think about those differences, the fact of who experiences them surely helps us to see not only how the subjective and objective differ, but also what makes those differences interesting – although, again, as with the Van Gogh example, interest is a subjective matter.

To repeat: what we assign our students to read is one of the most vital aspects of craft teaching. The logic is simple: craft teaching is about creating an experience that excites learning, and that experience involves far more than just what happens in the classroom. If the classroom is where you spark enthusiasm for much of what happens outside it, we need to remember that the process runs in two directions, and that what happens outside the classroom affects students' interest in coming back to class – or simply in learning.

One reason craft teaching needs to be particularly concerned with course readings is that these are what students use to "cover" the material. As I discussed in Chapter One, instilling enthusiasm for a subject matter requires instructors to let go of the perceived need to cover every one of their learning outcomes in class. For many, however, that suggestion is frightening. They worry that students cannot be trusted to learn the material on their own, without direct guidance. Truth be told, such a concern is far from misplaced: students often do *not* try to cover the material, or do so with enthusiasm neither for the subject at hand or for learning itself. I won't repeat my reasons for thinking we still are better off leaving coverage to the work done outside the classroom. I merely add the following: if we are going to rely more heavily on readings to do the work of covering the material (of "transferring knowledge"), then it becomes even more important to ensure that those readings cover the material in the most effective manner possible.

In thinking about the quantity of the course material, then, we also need to think about quality. I've suggested that the chief requirement of pedagogically sound readings is that they should *create*, not *presuppose*, students' interest in the subject. I've also suggested that clarity might be the single most effective way to do that. Learning is about being challenged, and in the face of a challenge, "getting something" is particularly rewarding – and confidence building. That fact puts clarity at a premium. These complementary requirements of clarity and sparking interest can be distilled into a simple litmus test: can students relate to what they are reading?[6]

Think again about my mathematic examples: both worked – for me, at least – because the explanations hung on a framework of actual life experience. I emphatically *cannot* relate to multiplying positive and negative numbers, as I cannot really even relate to negative *things*. "Negative things" seems like an oxymoron, as in nothing-something. Yet I *have* owed money. I can relate to *that*, and as soon as I saw this mathematical operation in that light, I finally got my head around it. It was the same with fractals. "Self-similarity" sounded vaguely redundant to me – hardly the basis for a firm understanding of anything. Yet I've seen cauliflower; I might even have noticed how it displayed the very phenomenon fractals describe. I can relate to cauliflower, and because of that fact, I can now relate to fractals.

I cannot say how this litmus test might affect the choices that you, the reader, make about the readings available in your discipline. My own experience has led me to avoid textbooks, but I do not doubt that in a variety of disciplines good ones are out there. Nor do I doubt why they are good: they transfer knowledge with the heavy use of simple and relatable examples; they hang explanations of the abstract on realities of the particular; they start with what students know, and move from there to what students do not yet know, but now *want* to know.

That said, there are good alternatives to textbooks. The most prominent are case studies: readings explicitly grounded in the priority of the familiar and knowable over the unfamiliar and seemingly unknowable. I have seen, especially in STEM education, how effectively students can grasp difficult abstractions only after reading cases that bring the reality of those abstractions to light. The coefficient of friction certainly makes more sense to someone who has first contemplated how stopping a car on a road differs from doing so on a frozen pond. If you teach in the tropics, you might, however, come up with another example.[7]

Slow Teaching: Technology, the Senses, and Learning

When technique enters into every area of life, including the human, it ceases to be external to man and becomes his very substance. It is no longer face to face with man but is integrated with him, and it progressively absorbs him.

– Jacques Ellul[1]

The Curse of Technology

As I argued in Chapter One, teaching, conceived of as a craft, is about motivating students to teach themselves. To accomplish that task, we need, of course, to capture their interest, both at a very general level – we want them to spend their lives engrossed in the subject we teach them – and also on a day-to-day basis – we want them to be engaged in class and on their assignments. One effective way to capture their interest is to raise their hackles – to get them invested in a subject by ... well ... irritating them. One must draw a fine line here: we want to challenge students, but we don't want to put them off. So, for instance, we might begin a discussion of gay marriage with the somewhat contentious claim that religion has no place in deciding which romantic unions governments should sanction. We would *not* begin that discussion, however, with an attack on religion. One discussion might put people on the defensive; the other is bound to actively offend them – with the likely result that they will simply tune us out.

I mention this strategy, and the tension involved with it, because I intend to employ it in this chapter. The subject is technology, about which, as you will see, I have some fairly strong views. In the end, these views are probably not all that significant with respect to the pedagogical point I want to make, but I raise them because they might serve the pedagogical purpose of getting you interested in that point – at least, I hope they serve that purpose: that's the issue at hand. My concern, and one reason I am revealing my strategy – which I would not do in the classroom – is that I might turn you off. In the classroom, I could navigate the tension in the room – that is, the extent to which I have gone too far and put students off – with the visual cues I was receiving. I have no such cues in writing, so, to be safe, a warning might be in order: I *want* to irritate at least some of you. Please know, however, that my purpose in doing so is to see if I can get across a message more effectively that, I trust, will *not* irritate you. Bear with me, then.

Another reason I am revealing my strategy is so that you can interrogate it as you go along. Think, as you read, not just about the substance of my words, but also about their pedagogical effect – their effect, that is, on your motivation to keep reading. Can you see how you might employ some version of this strategy? If so, what improvements might you make?

It might help, if you do get irritated, to bear in mind a point that you will see if you get to the end: I do not think that all technology is bad. Truly, I don't. What I can't accept, however, is that technology is – as it is so often treated – *the* solution. I don't accept either of these claims because, in truth, technology is not even the issue. The issue, rather, is summed up nicely in the famous words of Walt Kelly: "We have met the enemy and he is us."

So here goes …

I am, as my son once put it, technologically delayed. By that he meant that I inhabit the world of about 1974. I don't own an iPod or a Blackberry or a Bluetooth or a blueberry or any other fruit currently parading as a means of communication. I don't have a MyFace or a Spacebook page – nor do I have much of an idea what they are, although I'm pretty sure they're really bad things. I don't own a cell phone, and when people hand one to me I have no idea how to get it to do anything. The same is true of TV sets: after having lived without one for the past twenty years, I find I am no longer able to turn them on. What confuses me are all the remotes that people have lying about. They seem basically to be cell phones that call their TVs – though it seems an awfully short distance to be making a phone call. I never know which of these devices to pick up. In a recent attempt to turn on a friend's TV, I succeeded only in opening his garage door. We didn't know that at the time. The door stayed open all night and, poetically, some of his high-tech possessions were stolen.

The easiest, non-psychoanalytic explanation for my developmental delay is that cutting-edge gadgetry just doesn't excite me. This fact doesn't make me a better person, but I suspect it does explain a few of my more extreme and somewhat heretical educational views. To offer a few examples: I have come to the conclusion that PowerPoint is an affront to communication; in fact, it's an affront to thinking generally. I think "distance learning" – as in "online" learning – is a threat to human existence; the only distance that should occur in learning is between universities and distance learning.[2] I think e-books are a moral abomination – part of what John Updike nicely described as the "dephysicalization of experience"; books, he reminded us, provide ballast, if nothing else.

I don't actually hold all of these views, at least not in their absolute form. I do, however, like to say I do just to see how protective many educators are of the technological blanket in which they swath their professional lives. Insulting technology is much like insulting family and friends – in fact, that statement is probably more accurate without the "much like." And therein, I would argue, lies the problem that technology presents for education: it commands far more of our attention and allegiance than do the ends to which we put it. For many professors, technology itself has become the end, while education is simply a handy means. Such professors are not educators using technology; they are technologists using education.

Here, then, we see the instrumentalization of teaching at its extreme – extreme in the sense that any and all aspects of education have actually been dispensed with. In place of the excitement that education can, at its best, produce, we are left with the wonder of the new "app," the thrill of the dazzling visual presentation, the joy of the four-bar Internet connection. Such an inversion of our gaze goes unnoticed in a world where teaching already serves many masters. To the extent that we increasingly teach *to* things (for example, tests, marketable job skills) rather than simply *teach*, why would teaching *for* technological display (say, to show off our classroom response skills) strike us as being at all odd? For us to take any notice – for our technological inversion to come into focus – we would need a vision of teaching (of its activities and its methods) in which emerging technologies excite us only insofar as they serve pedagogical ends, rather than those of their own making.

Before we get to that vision, however, a few more words on the problem itself – in particular, how we got here. There are any number of explanations for academia's technological daze, first among them is that the world outside, which academics, to varying degrees, inhabit, is fixated on technological advances. More speculatively, technology offers something of which educators are in short supply: power – or at least its allure. Education can be a frustrating endeavor, as students do not always – and in some classes rarely – conform to our wishes. By contrast, technology offers the promise of control, of a world in which our actions bring about foreseeable effects. Such, after all, is the rationale of *all* advances in technique. It is no wonder that malfunctioning classroom technology is the source of extreme frustration. In such cases neither the students *nor* the technology are conforming to the instructor's will.

Of course, there are institutional factors at work, as administrators have – in roughly inverse proportion to their knowledge of education and in direct proportion to the amount of time since they themselves have set foot in a classroom – become serial enablers, using an approach that seems to say, "Here's the latest technology, go find a pedagogical use for it." (Imagine saying that about chalk.) The request is understandable, as it is far simpler to measure student learning by the bells and whistles present in a classroom than it is to attempt to gauge, say, critical thinking. In truth, of course, student learning is never measured at all, as, within this administrative world, technology becomes a proxy for legitimate educational outcomes and, eventually, the outcome itself – a fact that owes much to the tenuous research linking technology to various forms of student learning.[3] Think how bizarre it is that universities proudly offer tours of their empty state-of-the-art classrooms, as if learning can somehow be seen – in the overhead projector? – where no students are present. Not only are bells and whistles easier to measure than learning, they are easier to showcase.

And speaking of institutional constraints, we cannot forget about money. Armed with "Scantron" tests and virtual office hours, teachers can take on more students than ever before, and do so for far less than the cost of additional salaries. (Whether they can *teach* more students is another matter.) Throw into the mix technology companies that are to education what pharmaceutical companies are to medicine, and you arrive at a world in which teachers are daily bombarded with the latest, greatest technological way to present material, engage and assess[4] students, organize classes, and do just about anything else that was previously done with simpler technologies – pencils, chalk, and the like.[5]

Perhaps the most potent force in the push to be cutting edge is technology itself. Like the hair of a dog, various technologies have become the first line of defense against various other technologies, as teaching becomes something akin to an arms race. We deploy "clickers" and snazzy YouTube videos to capture the attention of Facebooking and texting students. We run papers through increasingly sophisticated cheating programs to defend against students who are using … increasingly sophisticated cheating programs. We search out the most effective "chat" software to facilitate discussions among students who never actually see one another because, *in light of such programs*, they are no longer required to.

The consequence of these and other factors is the creation of a mystique that, as I say, commands attention. The virtue of pencils and chalk is that they've been around long enough to be boring. As such, they do not beget technologists; teachers do not sit up at night conceiving of ways to use pencils or chalk. Not so with new technologies. In the rush to be wired, virtual, and cutting edge, we forget that being wired, virtual, or cutting edge might have little or nothing to do with students learning a damn thing. Moreover we overlook this problem precisely because technology has so effectively obscured it. In our technological mindset, concepts that aren't "PowerPointable" aren't teachable[6] (or even worth knowing), logging on to a classroom management system counts as engagement,[7] and finding the right app is a triumph of pedagogical imagination. These and other technologies no longer serve pedagogy; they now define it.[8]

That's a dramatic statement, so let me provide a couple of examples of what I mean. First, to pick on PowerPoint, the ubiquity of which makes it a worthy target:[9] the concern here is not that it allows professors to disseminate terabytes of information at rates far exceeding the capacity of anyone – students, conference participants, androids – to make very much of it.[10] The real concern is that the act of enabling that coverage makes doing so desirable and even necessary. Because instructors can move so quickly through the material, they see no reason *not* to. As a result, disseminating information – and lots of it – takes on a life of its own, as *coverage* becomes what teaching is. In a PowerPoint world, "I covered Chapter Five" somehow has become a pedagogical statement, one that to me sounds much like the tourist's claim to have "done" Paris (usually in no more than forty-eight hours).

Or consider the "chat" programs I mentioned above. These programs are designed to facilitate discussions outside the classroom. In principle this idea strikes me as a good one. I want my students to take any conversations they have in my classroom to their dorms or to cafes or to bars. The time they have in the classroom is never enough to address topics that can consume thoughtful people for an eternity. If they can't meet face to face, then having a virtual place to do so is great. I will even go so far as to say that, for some students, a virtual space might be preferable to a real one.[11]

What I have more difficulty with, however, is the notion of these virtual spaces *as* classrooms. What a classroom provides is precisely what the technological extremist prides himself on being able to eliminate: a public space. To be sure, virtual space can function in many of the same ways as an actual, physical classroom, but virtual space cannot be a classroom *conceptually*. Our conception of the classroom, as a place where Christian and atheist, gay and straight, redneck and hippy, black, white, and yellow can come together, hear what each has to say, and, in the process, create an intersubjective learning experience that brings the subject matter to life is one that, for the foreseeable future,[12] needs to remain tied to physical space. There might come a time when physical proximity no longer matters to human relations, including education – when emoticon-speak conveys meaning as accurately and transparently as a face-to-face encounter. (Perhaps all emotional states will be signaled and recognized with thousands of subtly distinct smiley faces. I can hardly wait. ☺) But we are not – contrary to whatever that little thing in your hand on which you keep typing tells you – there yet.[13]

Until we get there, the idea of a chat room as the new classroom only distorts educational reality by leading us to think that there is nothing lost in eliminating shared physical space.[14] Worse, the allure of the virtual classroom threatens to turn that physical space into an inconvenience, a luxury for which there is neither need nor time.[15] In the world of technology, elements of education that cry for no technological fix become liabilities.[16] Classrooms in particular become little more than rooms for improvement – places where students sleep, text, and have every ounce of curiosity sucked from them, if they show up at all.[17] In speaking endlessly about "what's really happening in the classroom," technologists entrench the conception that teachers are doing precisely what the technologists say they are. Moreover, once we all buy into the notion that this is what we're doing now, that this is all a lecture can be, we allow what we're doing to become the paradigm of bad teaching – something that can be improved only – surprise, surprise – by supplementing it with technology. Much like the adroit advertiser, technologists pathologize the normal and then come to our rescue with the cure.

There are, of course, bad uses of classrooms. In a sense, that's the point: there's clearly work to be done. But *what* work? Is it technological or *pedagogical*? Think about it this way: can you imagine a technology policy in which specific classrooms are actively *un*wired (or perhaps where cell phone reception is jammed) so that students are no longer able to get online? After all, if learning is really the goal, why not make classrooms available where instructors who so choose can promote that end in the absence of technological distraction? The demand for such a space exists, as many faculty already ban cell phone and laptop use in their classrooms. But where is the administrative support?

The answer is that such support is lost in the same goal-inverting technological fog that envelops much of the rest of academia.[18] In this fog all pedagogical questions yield technological answers – answers whose content is algorithmically preordained. Plug in any query: should we, in our high-speed world, seek to reclaim the intimacy and relative calm of physical encounters, or should we jump on board and forsake both in favor of alluring virtual ones? And if we do preserve our physical encounters, should we explore further their social possibilities, or should we seek to mediate them into oblivion with a glitzy Prezi show or (yet another) raucous round of clicker fun? We know the answers to such questions because we know the program. We know, in other words, that the future is now and the present is gone.

Okay, I'm done. Things might have gotten somewhat out of hand. I confess that beyond a certain point my enthusiasm just kept building to a crescendo whose peak even I didn't see coming. I suppose I could have gone back and toned it down a bit. I'd certainly have done more to acknowledge, for example, that there are important class cleavages to consider: for some, technological advances get around the time and financial constraints that education imposes – although recent studies show that the extent to which technology has enabled lower-income people to get an education is much less than predicted.[19] I did not tone down my outburst, however, for the reason I gave at the outset: I'm interested to know how, as a pedagogical matter, any irritation you might have felt at my somewhat loose and polemical style affected your inclination to read on. I wanted you to become invested, but not alienated, and as different people draw that line in different places, I probably did a bit of both. To both groups, I ask the key question: what are the pedagogical limits of irritation? If you were irritated, why – for some of you – did your irritation motivate you to read further, and why – for the rest of you – did it tempt you to quit altogether? (If you're reading these words, I assume you did not give into temptation.) If you felt no irritation – if my rant was music to your ears – did reading the views of a kindred spirit affect your motivation to learn?

To *all* who got this far, turn now to Part Two, which I separate from the preceding discussion to underscore a fairly abrupt change of tone. I've had my rant, and I enjoyed it, but now I intend to say something constructive.

Recovery

To say that we occupy a PowerPoint world or that we are in a technology stupor is to suggest that gaining perspective is no small matter. How critical can our gaze upon technology be if our frame of reference is technologically imbued? Indeed, gaining perspective *on* technology from within a technological world presents a classic problem of social determinacy: if social structures determine consciousness, how can there be reflection on, and critical reform of, those structures?

Fortunately this classic problem is more apparent than real, as no social theorist I can name would really argue for words like "determinacy" and "determine" to be taken in an absolute sense. Jacques Ellul, whose ominous words began this chapter and who might be thought of as the father of technological determinism, himself insisted that sociological analysis had little to say about the actions of individuals. Thus, he observed, "[i]f we do not even consider the possibility of making a stand against these determinants, then everything *will* happen as I have described it, and the determinants *will* be transformed into inevitabilities."[20] The first step in that stand is not to reject *techniques* – as if that were an option – but simply to reflect on the manner in which they divert our focus from the ends of education (teaching and learning) to its means. I have engaged in such reflection here, but only at an abstract level. The task for educators is to reflect at a much more immediate level: how does our excitement about technology creep into and perhaps change our actual, everyday thinking – the thinking we do when we prepare for this Tuesday's lecture on Chaucer or next Monday's seminar on property law?

One way of answering this question is to consider what it would look like to teach *without* technology at the forefront of our thoughts. How would it be different if *teaching* – and, yes, student learning – rather than the use of technology, were restored to its rightful place as our objective? I do not mean how would the classroom itself be different. My interest has more to do with the thoughts we have before entering the classroom: how would we prepare to teach a certain topic if we put the craft of teaching at the forefront of our thoughts and allowed the technological tools of that craft only the supporting role they are due?

What follows is at least a partial answer to these questions, given by way of two versions of a mock lecture. The topic of this lecture is well outside my own academic discipline. I chose it because it is, while conceptually challenging, singular in its focus. This fact is important: in the end, my concern is not the subject matter itself but considerations of how to teach it. These considerations come in two layers. On the surface are the pedagogical techniques we choose. Below is the matter – of greater interest, in my mind – of how we come to choose them. Generally speaking, for any given subject on any given day in any given classroom, any number of techniques could be effective and for any number of reasons. Much depends on what an instructor is comfortable with, as some techniques are surely better suited to some types of people (as I discussed in Chapter Two on teaching personas). Yet, although there might be no one right technique, there is, I would argue, a right way to think through our decision.

The following, then, is an illustration of how that thinking might proceed. The illustration is limited in several ways. First, my focus is on high-tech techniques. (If that sounds redundant, then you have drunk too much technological Kool-Aid.) Second, the pedagogical goal here is narrow, as I am interested only in how one might explain a difficult concept. Hence I leave aside for now my emphasis on teaching as generating enthusiasm *about* concepts. Finally, much of what I have to say is with respect to two senses – sight and sound – through which students learn. Not only are other senses important to learning, so too are non-sensory aspects of education (emotional attachment, for instance). For now, I set them aside.

As you read the description of this mini-lecture, try to put yourself in the shoes of a student witnessing it. What are you seeing? What are you hearing? What do you understand? What do you *not* understand? Above all, keep in mind the following crucial fact: I, your professor, am merely standing and talking. I am not writing anything down on a board or using any sort of projected images. (The term for this is teaching naked – a telling term, for it implies that technology, like clothing, is all that stands between an instructor and unbearable shame and humiliation.) Technology still exists – the students sit in chairs and there is a roof over our heads – and yet it has slid seamlessly into our collective unconscious. Without further ado, let us begin:

> *Welcome. The lesson today is entitled "Prime Numbers and Their Limits." There are two principal objectives of this lesson – the first is to understand what prime numbers are, and the second is to see if we can understand a few of their more interesting properties. Let me begin by asking – who knows what a prime number is?*

At this point I call on perhaps two or three students to explain to the class that a prime number is a number that is divisible only by itself and 1. After this, I continue on:

> *I want to highlight two facts about prime numbers. First, they are the building blocks of all other numbers: all numbers are reducible to primes. For example, 42 can be broken down to 2 x 21, which in turn can be broken down to 2 x 3 x 7, at which point, we're done – we can go no further. Similarly, 666 ends up as a multiple of 2, 3, 3, and 37. Someone throw out another number and let's see how it works.*

Here I repeat this process of breaking down numbers into primes as many times as I think are needed for everyone to grasp the idea.

> *Okay, that's the first fact about primes, they're building blocks. The second interesting fact about them is that their frequency decreases as numbers (integers technically) get larger. One way of seeing this is that, in the first 10 numbers, 1 in 2.5 is prime (4 out of the 10); in the first 100, 1 in 4; in the first 1,000, 1 in 6; the first 10,000, 1 in 8.1; the first 100,000, 1 in 10.4. Another way to see it is that, in the first 1,000 positive numbers, 168 are prime; in the second 1,000, 135 are prime; in the third, 127; fourth, 120; fifth, 119; and the last five chunks of thousands before 10 million have 62, 58, 67, 64, and 53 primes.*

Now that we know something about primes, here's the big question: do you suppose they go on forever or do you think they eventually stop altogether? Raise your hand if you know the answer with 100 percent certainty.

I pause, and wait long enough for a smattering of hands to appear.

Now, those of you who didn't raise your hand, what makes intuitive sense to you – go on forever or stop?

A common intuition is that they'd have to stop. As students will note in their responses, not only is the frequency of primes decreasing, but sooner or later the numbers get so large that, one would think, *something* would have to go into them (besides themselves and 1). How could a hundred-digit number not be divisible by *something*?

Now, those of you who did raise your hand, what are your answers?

After I get a few responses – without justifications – I ask,

Could you prove it?

And here I stop to discuss the difference between knowing something intuitively ("it just feels like primes would have to go on forever") or empirically ("they just keep finding larger primes") and knowing it in the conclusive, theoretical sense – a sense that comes with having proven it *always* to be the case.[21]

Now it turns out we've known the answer for thousands of years, because Euclid demonstrated it. Here's how he did it.[22] He started by saying, "Let's suppose prime numbers stop; suppose there is a finite number of them. If that's the case, what would happen if we multiplied all those primes together, then added one to the number we got?"

Here I might stop to point something out:

> *Before you answer that question, think about the following. If you mul-*
> *tiply any numbers greater than 1 together and add 1 to the product, the*
> *result would not be divisible by any of the numbers you had multiplied. It*
> *would not be divisible for the simple reason that, to get from the product of*
> *those numbers to the next number that was divisible by any of them, you*
> *would have to add that number.* (I might repeat that sentence. Feel free
> to reread it.) *Given, however, that the numbers are larger than 1, adding*
> *only 1 won't do the trick.*
>
>   *For example, when we multiply 3 by 7 and get 21, we know that the next*
> *number after 21 that is divisible by 3 must be 21 plus 3, and the next num-*
> *ber after 21 that is divisible by 7 must be 21 plus 7. Simply adding 1 to 21*
> *doesn't take us far enough to get to the next multiple of 3 or 7. It might be*
> *divisible by other numbers – as 22 is by 2 and 11 – but that's another mat-*
> *ter. The key point is that by adding 1 to our product we reach a number that*
> *can't be divisible by the numbers we used to get to it. Does that make sense?*

After making any necessary clarifications, I proceed:

> *Now let's go back to our question: if there were a finite number of primes*
> *and we multiplied them by each other and added 1 to the product, what*
> *could we say about this (very large) number?*

Students – to the extent that they have understood the previous
discussion – point out that this number must not be divisible by any of
the primes.

> *But remember what we said – all numbers are reducible to primes! So what*
> *follows from this? Ideas?*

At this point I ask around until I elicit something close to the following
answer: either *this* number is a prime or, if it isn't, there must be some

other prime or primes – not in our initial list – to which it can be reduced. Either way, our initial claim that we had all the primes was false.

> *That's right – very good! Moreover that initial claim always has to be false, because every time we assume it to be true, the same logic will undermine it. And so the answer to our question is: primes have to go on forever. We now have* proof *of that fact.*

I then close the mini-lecture by commenting, quite genuinely:

> *I love this proof. It's so elegant and so simple and so powerful. I think all academics should aspire to that kind of beauty.*[23]

If I have thirty-odd seconds remaining, I might also remark:

> *This is a wonderful example of how to prove a point by demonstrating that its negation leads to contradiction, what we call a* reductio ad absurdum – *about which G.H. Hardy remarked: "It is a far finer gambit than any chess gambit: a chess player may offer the sacrifice of a pawn or even a piece, but a mathematician offers* the game."[24]

End of lesson. If, in reading my description, you managed actually to put yourself in my students' shoes and conceptualize it as they might have, you might have concluded that many of them would have been confused. If you did not draw that conclusion – if you thought that they'd have got it – it is possible and, I would maintain, even likely that you cheated and viewed the explanation from a perspective the students were not offered. I say that for an obvious reason: you *read* the description, rather than *listened* to it, so you were able to *see* certain conceptual points because they were written on the page in front of you. The students would have had no such vantage point. For them, the lesson was purely aural; I never once wrote anything on the board or showed them an overhead slide. Granted, what you saw was not particularly illuminating, but concepts on a page offer at least a slight analytic reference not offered by ones merely held in your head. More significantly, you had a temporal advantage: readers can read as slowly and as many times as is required for them to understand. In listening to my explanation, students had to go at my pace.

In short, you could not possibly have complied with my request to "put yourself in the shoes of a student." I tricked you. In seeing something the students could not, you experienced learning in a manner they could not. And that's the point: the shoes in which we find ourselves are determined by the nature of the experience we are having. If we accept that fact – and it is difficult to deny something that borders on a truism – then the pedagogical question becomes: how might students best *experience* a concept or idea or argument or fact – or *anything* – that we wish them to grasp?

What this question points to is the need to think about the relationship between the concept to be learned and the sorts of experiences through which students can be introduced to it. Whereas we might, in considering the concept, think only in straightforwardly analytic terms – as in, "here's a concept, here's what it means, here's an example" – we might instead ask, for any given concept, "what sort of educational experience would allow students to grasp it at the level we wish?"[25]

This question leads us back to the matter of pedagogical techniques, which we should think of as the bag of tools with which we create educational experiences. Teaching a concept then becomes a matter of first deciding which experiences are best for the concept we have in mind, and then – and *only* then – deciding which tools are best for creating that experience.[26] A good example of what I'm talking about is Euclid's proof: ask yourself in what way even the meager visual representation of the proof that you got from reading it made your experience different from that of the hypothetical students? In what way(s) did having visual cues give you a distinct advantage in conceptualizing the infinite nature of primes?

To illustrate, let's break the lesson down into its individual conceptual points, and examine in each case whether the pedagogical technique I used created an experience that would help students understand. The first conceptual point concerned the nature of a prime number. The pedagogical technique I used to explain this concept was student participation and discussion. Was it effective? Perhaps: the technique is certainly valuable in that it provides students the experience of hearing the explanation from those whose language, conceptual framework, and mode of expression they might grasp more readily than a professor's. Students often provide explanations that professors, with more advanced levels of understanding, would never consider. (I elaborate on this point in Chapter Two.) Having more than one student respond is an effective way to ensure that a maximum number of them will have heard an explanation that made sense to them or, as is more likely, that they will have grasped the concept from the overlap of the multiple explanations. There is also the advantage to me of being able to use the students' comments to gauge their grasp of the concept. If I did not elicit comments, I would have no way of knowing (except perhaps from body language) whether their level of understanding was adequate for moving to the next stage.

So hearing from students and providing them a forum to hear from one another – these were the components of the learning experience I used. Note that there were no visual aspects to this experience. Should there have been? Perhaps, but as it is not immediately apparent that *seeing* 11 or 83 would help us to understand why they are prime, adding a visual component probably would not bring much to the experience, and might actually serve as a distraction. (That said, I *am* implying that the ability of you, the reader, to see the numbers might have helped, so I can't definitively reject the idea that a visual aid could be useful.)

I am not suggesting my discussion was anything more than one among many possible strategies – the use of small groups comes to mind, for instance. Nevertheless, let us assume for argument's sake that the experience I chose to create was, from a pedagogical standpoint, a plausible one. The question that remains is whether the means of bringing that experience about could be improved. And here we might reasonably ask: could technology help? Could it enhance the experience of hearing student voices? Classroom response systems ("clickers" – if you don't know what they are, ask your tech people) might provide a good introduction to the idea, at least in terms of gauging students' grasp of the concept. Moreover they would provide a diversion, a way of briefly shifting focus away from the discussion. In this way, even if they didn't add any pedagogical value of their own, they might – by recharging students' energy levels – add such value to whatever they provide a break from (in this case, the discussion).

That said, the situation does not cry out for an obvious technological fix. I'll grant, however, that I could be missing something. Tech-savvy readers, assuming they didn't stop reading a few pages back, have no doubt already come up with many great ideas. Let me just make two points before moving on. First, if we do add technology, we ought to do so only with the assurance that it will not in some way undermine the experience that our discussion provides. To pick an absurd example, asking students to text each other rather than talk directly would be strange. They can text all they like outside class, so why would we not resort to the form of communication that might be unavailable to them during the week? At a less absurd level, even the clickers, to the extent they take time away from the discussion, might be intrusive. And with regard to giving students a diversionary break, it is far from obvious that one was necessary given that this discussion took place within the first five minutes, when attention spans had not yet been stretched to the breaking point.

The second point is that the choice of technology is not really the issue anyway – the *timing* of the choice is: we ask about technology *only after* we have decided on the experience we wish to provide. We do not decide on the technology and let that decision dictate the experience; we decide on the experience and then find (or not) a technology that might help us create this experience. In this manner, we constrain the technology decision with a clear litmus test: will it – whatever form "it" takes – enhance the experience we *already* have in mind?

Let us move now to the next two conceptual points: prime numbers as building blocks of all numbers and their diminishing frequency. The students' experience here was that of passive listening – listening to my explanations of both ideas. To simplify matters, let's suppose that the experience was generally acceptable. I can think of many ways in which the experience could have been more active, but let's merely ask how this passive experience might have been enhanced. What pedagogical tools might I have employed? Here I think that at least one visual aid would have helped, one that might have made the diminishing frequency of primes more obvious. Numerical frequency is, or at least can be conceived of as, a spatial concept, one that can be represented with a number line or, alternatively, a graphic depiction. Figure 1 offers an example.

No matter what we might think about the figure's conceptually illuminating power, the pedagogical point is simply that my decision to use, say, a PowerPoint or overhead slide to supplement my verbal explanation was one that came only *after* I had decided on the general nature of the classroom experience – namely, that it should have a visual component. I did not first see the graphic and wonder what purpose it might serve. To the contrary, I saw a conceptual challenge and wondered what tool might serve *it*.

The aspect of the lesson that was perhaps in most need of some form of visual aid was what came next: Euclid's proof. As with the conceptual points on prime numbers, my teaching technique here was not much of a technique at all – I just tried to explain the proof verbally. Yet to an even greater degree this conceptual step needed to be *seen,* not just heard, to be understood.[27] Such a need might not be the same for all students, but it is certainly the case that visualization is, for many people, an important element to understanding, even perhaps at the highest

Figure 1. The Frequency of Prime Numbers

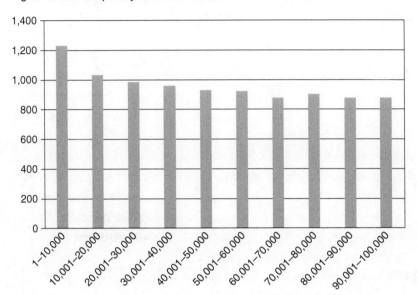

levels – and even those who don't need visual representation might benefit by having a break from the aural.[28] Take, for instance, the brief explanation of why adding 1 to the product of any numbers yields a number that is not divisible by those numbers. This concept might be difficult for many to follow for the simple reason that they cannot keep numbers in their head. (Notice that keeping numbers in one's head means not making them visual in the sense of being concurrently perceptible by more than one person.) To alleviate that problem, let us rewind the tape and introduce one of my favorite – no surprise, perhaps – forms of technology: the blackboard.[29]

If you are getting bored by now, I don't blame you. Reading this is different from seeing an instructor before you in a classroom. There was also the stuff in the beginning, dumping on technology. So it's been a pretty long class, and as this is a book, I can't exactly switch media on you. I suggest that you take a break and come back. Seriously, your span of concentration must have been surpassed back when I started lamenting the decline of pencils and chalk. At least get up and stretch. It's good for your back if nothing else.

Back to blackboards. I like them for many reasons, chief among them that they limit the pace – a crucial aspect of the learning experience – at which an instructor can present material. Writing out words can be slow, but oddly enough it takes roughly the same time for an instructor to write out a word as it does for a student to do so. The immediate virtue of the blackboard, then, is that it puts teacher and learner on the same temporal plane. By contrast, a PowerPoint or overhead slide puts the students and the instructor on very different planes, as each slide can pack in three to five minutes of required writing time, but might be displayed for less than half that time.[30] (Of course, transcribing them might not be desired, but if that's the case tell your students beforehand.)

There is also another temporal issue to consider. In discussing PowerPoint at a faculty seminar recently, a participant told me of a casual experiment she had tried in her class. In two consecutive classes, she first presented the material with PowerPoint and in the next class with a whiteboard, and reported that about twice as many students preferred the whiteboard to PowerPoint. What struck me more than this admittedly unscientific[31] result was one of the reasons students gave for preferring the whiteboard: in seeing her work through the material in real time, they felt she was doing it *with* them. She seemed more present to them, more engaged. It was not just that she was working through material at the same *rate*; she was actually doing it *at the same time*, adding an additional layer of synchronicity. In this way, she did not simply *seem* more present, she actually was. By contrast, reading PowerPoint slides while thinking about what to make for dinner is possible; it is not hard, however, for students to detect the lack of presence, even if they do so only at an unconscious level.[32] Think of it this way: a PowerPoint slide contains a professor's embedded labor – the labor that went into making it. This labor, days or months or years old, remains hidden from anyone viewing the slide. Students see the answer (it is unleashed on them), but not the process that led to it: the thought, but not the thinking. As a metaphor, consider that the embedded labor and knowledge in a PowerPoint slide is much like the energy embedded in fossil fuels – energy that, when combusted, is released at a rate far faster than the original matter was created. Writing thoughts out on the board, then, not only slows the pace of our thoughts, it reveals aspects of the process that, in our rush to "cover" the material, we fail to appreciate as being integral parts of learning.

Okay – back to my class, and, specifically, to the explanation of why adding 1 to the product of any numbers yields a number that is not divisible by those numbers. With the blackboard in place, I could draw a number line that shaded intervals of, say, 3. It might look like Figure 2.

Figure 2. Intervals of 3

I could then point out that, if you travel 1 past any of the multiples (3, 6, 9, …), you arrive at a number (4, 7, 10, …) that is not divisible by 3 for the simple reason that you have not traveled far enough to have added another 3. "Travel" implies distance, and although numbers have no actual distance to them – they take up no space and as such are not physical – presenting them on a number line embodies them in such a fashion as to give them distance. In the process, we give students something to visualize.

The next step is to add another number – say, 5; I said 7 before, but 5 fits more easily on the board – to demonstrate graphically what happens when we multiply numbers together. The number line might look like Figure 3.

Figure 3. Intervals of 5 and 3

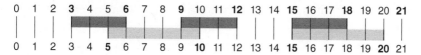

Here I would draw students' attention to 15, the multiple of my two numbers, and ask them what happens if I move 1 past 15 to 16. I could ask: have I traveled far enough to get to a number that is divisible by either 3 or 5? Clearly I have not – to do that I would need to travel either 3 or 5 segments. Visualized as such, the effect of adding 1 to the multiple of any numbers (again, integers technically) greater than 1 would be clear: students could *see* that it would not get us to another multiple, that the number we reached (16, in my example) could not be divisible by the numbers we multiplied together. (See Figure 4.)

Figure 4. Three 5s + 1

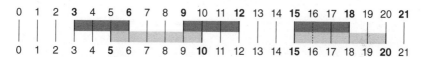

As soon as students caught on to this idea, I could move seamlessly to what happens when, assuming there is a finite amount of primes, we multiply them all together and add 1. And here – so that I can use the graphic I have already drawn – I might employ a slight fiction, asking them to imagine that 3 and 5 comprise the set of all primes. Looking at the number line, they need only remind themselves that, when we multiply them together and add 1, the number we get could not be divisible by 3 or 5 (my fictional set of all primes).

The existence of 16 – a number that is not divisible by my primes and therefore must either be prime or, as we know in this case, divisible by another prime, 2 – demonstrates that there could *never* be a complete set of all primes, as adding 1 to the multiple of them would *always* bring us to a number that requires the existence of at least one other prime.

So there it is – we're done. You still might not have grasped it, and in that regard you might have something in common with the students you were imagining. The point, however, is not that any one educational method is a foolproof way of explaining a concept, much less of generating enthusiasm for it. It's not the method itself, but the thinking that leads us to it. If my students failed to grasp the infinite nature of primes, it is because the experience I provided them was not up to the task. But in that case the method was not the problem – it might be right in some other context. The problem was with the deliberations that led me to adopt that method. With those deliberations lay the success or failure of the lesson. Imagine, then, how perilous it is to adopt a technology in the absence of *any* such deliberation.

Before moving on to a few conclusions, I cannot resist a quick historical aside. The interesting thing about my strategy of adding physical dimensions to numbers so as to allow students to visualize them is that it follows the strategy Euclid himself employed. (You can indulge your technological urges and look it up on the Internet.) In fact, the initial explanation I gave of the proof was actually in a language that Euclid did not speak and that would not be spoken in the West for more than a millennium. In Euclid's day geometry was the language of mathematics. (It has since become indistinguishable from Euclid himself – since Einstein we have referred to the geometry we learned in high school as *Euclidian* geometry.) Even where Euclid dabbled in number theory, he did so with shapes and lines – *visual* forms that are not just representations of things, but the things themselves.

With the advent of algebra and number theory generally, mathematics shifted from *things* to the *representation* of things, with the thing itself hidden from view.[33] $x^2 + 2x$ is an idea, one that I have just represented on the page. As such, it differs greatly, for example, from a number line in which $(x + 2)$ x's are drawn out.[34] Thought of in this manner, we might say that the advent of algebra marked not just a conceptual shift of the mathematical world, but also a major pedagogical shift. The two always go hand in hand, of course – as I argued in the Preface, the distinctions we make between the production of knowledge and its dissemination through teaching are well overblown – but conceptual changes do not always involve such radical shifts in our manner of perception. To go from a visual language such as geometry to a non-visual, representational one such as algebra is indeed radical, given the importance of the visual for so many, and must at least partially explain why many students who have difficulty with algebra excel in geometry. In short, what separates the two disciplines for many students might be less a matter of the required analytic skills than simply the fact that they lend themselves to entirely different learning experiences.[35] If any observation speaks to the importance of giving due consideration to the classroom experiences we create, it is that.

At first glance, the moral of the story is disarmingly simple: think first about the concepts that need explaining, then go to the classroom experiences best suited to that task, and then – *and only then* – think about whether a certain technology might help. This temporal order reflects a crucial hierarchy, one in which pedagogy drives technology, not the other way around. If that rule seems too banal even to mention, ask yourself, the next time you prepare for a class, why you uploaded PowerPoint (or Prezi or any other such visual aid) before you stopped to consider the subject at hand. Simple though it might be, the inversion can only really be seen if a certain understanding of teaching – *teaching as an end and as a craft, not as a means to an end beyond our choosing* – is the object of our gaze.

We can, however, more deeply entrench pedagogy's priority if we take the temporal sequence further: after introducing a technological innovation, take a moment after class to reflect on its impact. In particular, ask the following: did the technology increase student engagement? did it foster constructive interaction among students and/or between the students and you? did it increase your ability to engage a diversity of learning styles?[36] did it have a positive impact on the use of class time, on course preparation time, on course management time? did it, most importantly, help to generate excitement in learning? In all of these questions the major practical consideration to keep in mind is that the classroom should be adding a social element to the course, so it is vital that whatever technology you use promote, rather than inhibit, that purpose.

While I stand by my simple moral, I should emphasize that, in at least one respect, it *is* simple: in reality the technological aspects of education cannot be isolated and examined in a detached manner; to do so is to forget just how technologically determined the entire context is. When we think now – in the twenty-first century – about concepts that are important and about the classroom experience and pedagogical strategies we need for explaining them, our thoughts on both issues are colored by ways of knowing and ways of communicating that are themselves part and parcel of the technology by which we are surrounded. As I suggested earlier, we can look circumspectly on the technology we employ, but we should not delude ourselves that our view will be unfiltered and unmediated by it. Circumspection means looking *around*, not looking through.

When technological advances are vilified, it is usually for the ways they alter our grasp of reality and our ways of communicating. Ultimately, though, they do what they do, with the result that we become people who know the world and communicate with one another on different terms than we did before. It is, however, *this* way of knowing the world and communicating with others that we educators must accept as our starting point if we are to promote learning. Colleagues of mine constantly lament what the cell phone and the laptop have done to their classes. My reply is that, after we are through lamenting that fact, we must then try to figure out how students who are wedded to their cell phones and laptops might learn.[37] In other words, we can despair of technological change, but then we need to get over it. It certainly makes little sense to devise learning activities with clay-tablet-wielding students in mind.

Saying this, however, does not change the essential fact that the goal is to generate excitement about learning; technology is merely a tool we might use to achieve it. And it certainly does not change the more general moral of the chapter: teaching, like all crafts, has tools, but when the tools become the main attraction, the craft ceases to exist. The fault, however, lies not with the tools. My target here is certainly not PowerPoint or clickers or laptops; whatever issues I have with individual technologies are beside the point. What matters is the mode of thinking that puts them at center stage. When technologies create problems in the classroom, it is because they are introduced without enough thought given to how – *concretely, actually* – they are expected to help students learn. This statement is as true of chalk as it is of laptops.

Why You Should Ignore Cheating

What *Is* Cheating?

When I was in high school I cheated, and I did so on more than one occasion. Most of those occasions were in my US history class. The day before a test, our teacher would lecture at great length about a certain topic, sprinkling his remarks with, "Now if I were to ask you to write an essay on this, I'd want you to be sure to mention …" By the end of class, there was no doubt what the next day's essay question would be or about what would constitute a good answer. The only doubt that remained was whether he would tell us, as we walked into class, that the test should be written on our own paper or whether he would instead hand out a blue or a green examination booklet. Those were the only three options – *ever*. (He had been assessing students in this manner for as long as anyone could remember.)

I am not exaggerating when I say that most students did the same thing I did the night before the test: we wrote out our answers to the essay question on blue examination booklets as well as green ones and on our own pieces of paper. The following day we simply handed in the medium du jour at the end of class. The only real chore, besides being somewhat discreet in replacing empty booklets or paper with filled ones before handing them in, was to figure out what to do with ourselves for the fifty minutes we were supposed to be writing. I often found that the easiest thing to do was simply to write out the essay yet again. Having written it three times the night before, it wasn't hard, and there was the added advantage of not having to go through the delicate switching. On those days, I suppose technically no cheating occurred, but there were plenty of other days in which I simply passed notes to others for the fifty minutes and handed in the prepackaged goods at the bell.

Thinking back on this episode in my academic career, I confess I don't feel a lot of remorse.[1] I learned something writing out those essays: repetition, it turns out, is a central component to learning. And my dishonesty didn't come at anyone's expense – grades were not on a scale. In fact I have often wondered whether I was deceiving my teacher or he me. It is difficult to believe he was not aware of the implications of the time-honored ritual he had created, and it seems at least possible that his testing technique was simply a clever pedagogical ploy in which the impulse to cheat was channeled into a learning experience. We cheaters perhaps did better on the tests than many of our honest classmates, but my sense is that in the process we also might have learned more than they did. In other words, we learned more and got higher grades, which comes pretty close to reflecting what grades are supposed to be about.

Here's the question: let's say it was a pedagogical ploy – was it a good one? Is this the sort of ploy that indicates the elevation of teaching to a craft? Is it a really a craft when we *lure* students into cheating – when we actually offer them an incentive to do it? My first thought is yes, to all the above. In what follows, we'll see how that first thought holds up. To cut to the conclusion, I will raise a few concerns about cheating as a means to learning – although perhaps not the ones you might be thinking about – but in the end I'm not sure I can rule this, or any, strategy out altogether.

To explain my position, let's begin with an exercise that I often use in workshops on cheating. It came originally from Fredrick Crews, though I learned of it via Barbara Davis's classic *Tools for Teaching*.[2] It involves more history, in this case the practice – more dubious than my own, or so

I would argue – of falsely claiming credit for other people's ideas. To begin, read the following passage from *History of the World*, by J.M. Roberts:[3]

> The joker in the European pack was Italy. For a time hopes were entertained of her as a force against Germany, but these disappeared under Mussolini. In 1935 Italy made a belated attempt to participate in the scramble for Africa by invading Ethiopia. It was clearly a breach of the covenant of the League of Nations for one of its members to attack another. France and Great Britain, as great powers, Mediterranean powers, and African colonial powers, were bound to take the lead against Italy at the league. But they did so feebly and half-heartedly because they did not want to alienate a possible ally against Germany. The result was the worst possible: the league failed to check aggression, Ethiopia lost her independence, and Italy was alienated after all.

Now suppose you, as a European history teacher, assigned students a paper in which they were to provide an analysis of the lead-up to the Second World War, and suppose further that one of the papers you received contained the following passage:

> Italy, one might say, was the joker in the European deck. When she invaded Ethiopia, it was clearly a breach of the covenant of the League of Nations; yet the efforts of England and France to take the lead against her were feeble and half-hearted. It appears that those great powers had no wish to alienate a possible ally against Hitler's rearmed Germany.
>
> (No citations provided)

Bearing in mind that no citations were provided, is the passage an example of plagiarism, yes or no? (Answer to follow.) And here's one other question before we move on to a second example of student work: how would you characterize your level of certainty about your answer: high, medium, or no real clue?

Now look at a slightly different passage:

Italy was the joker of the European deck. Under Mussolini in 1935, she made a belated attempt to participate in the scramble for Africa by invading Ethiopia. As J.M. Roberts points out, this violated the covenant of the League of Nations.[1] But France and Britain, not wanting to alienate a possible ally against Germany, put up only a feeble and half-hearted opposition to the Ethiopian adventure. The outcome, as Roberts observes, was "the worst possible: the league failed to check aggression, Ethiopia lost her independence, and Italy was alienated after all."[2]

[1] J.M. Roberts, *History of the World* (New York: Knopf, 1976), p. 845.
[2] Roberts, p. 845.

Once again, is it plagiarism or not, and how certain are you of your answer?

Finally, student paper number three:

Much has been written about German rearmament and militarism in the period 1933–1939. But Germany's dominance in Europe was by no means a foregone conclusion. The fact is that the balance of power might have been tipped against Hitler if one or two things had turned out differently. Take Italy's gravitation toward an alliance with Germany, for example. That alliance seemed so very far from inevitable that Britain and France actually muted their criticism of the Ethiopian invasion in the hope of remaining friends with Italy. They opposed the Italians in the League of Nations, as J.M. Roberts observes, "feebly and half-heartedly because they did not want to alienate a possible ally against Germany."[1] Suppose Italy, France, and Britain had retained a certain common interest. Would Hitler have been able to get away with remarkable bluffing and bullying in the later thirties?

[1] J.M. Roberts, *History of the World* (New York: Knopf, 1976), p. 845.

Plagiarism? Degree of certainty?

Okay, let's get to the answers. Most people would say that the first passage is plagiarism and that they are highly certain of it. They are correct. But what, exactly, has the student wrongfully taken from Roberts? Clearly she has taken knowledge of facts: Italy invaded Ethiopia, the invasion was a breach of the covenant of the League of Nations. But is that why the passage is plagiarism? In fact, it is not. Roberts cannot claim ownership of such knowledge, as both the facts and knowledge about them are public. What is not public, however – what Roberts *does* own – is the manner in which these public facts are expressed. Roberts's turns of phrase are his, in the same manner that Chaucer's are his, and the student's sly interweaving of her own words with those of Roberts does not alter that fact.

Now let's look at the second passage. If you answered that this passage was also plagiarism, you are correct. The two correct citations of Roberts serve as a kind of alibi for the appropriating of other, unacknowledged phrases, but the alibi doesn't help, as some of Roberts's own words are again being presented as the student's. In addition the student has taken something else from Roberts – namely, his ideas *about* public facts. Historians do more than simply report fact – they interpret it, and those interpretations are theirs. Here we enter a slightly gray area, however, as interpretations sometimes can become public fact, and in any case, the line between fact and interpretation is not always clear. Look at statements such as "France and Great Britain ... were bound to take the lead against Italy at the league ..." or "they did so feebly and half-heartedly because they did not want to alienate a possible ally against Germany." Are these conjecture, belonging to Roberts, or indisputable historical truth, belonging to no one (bearing in mind that the wording *does* belong to Roberts)? Perhaps historians have a standard answer to such a question, but do all history professors know that answer? And, more to the point, do all history *students* know it?

Put these questions aside for a moment and look at the final passage. Here we have no plagiarism. The student has been influenced by the public facts mentioned by Roberts, but hasn't tried to pass off Roberts's conclusions as his own. The one clear borrowing is properly acknowledged. Did you get it right? How sure were you of your answer? For that matter, how sure were you of all your answers? Be honest: had you ever really considered that historians do not own public facts or that the two things to which they do have rights (the two things students cannot take without attribution) are the manner in which they express those – or any – facts and their interpretations of them? And do you have a sure-fire technique for distinguishing between facts and interpretations, and could you explain that technique to your students?

Let me admit that I cannot answer the first part of the last question in the affirmative, and if I could I am not sure I would have an affirmative answer to the second part. You might be better than I on these matters, but I suspect I am not alone in my inabilities.[4] And if I am not alone, then what does that say about academic dishonesty? Minimally it suggests that there is an area of moral ambiguity here – that there are degrees of cheating as well as degrees to which students and even professors are able to identify it.[5] One way to consider this conclusion is to think back to student #2 and ask yourself what sort of psychological profile you might give him. When I ask this question at workshops, faculty are usually fairly evenly divided. One group says he's conniving, that his proper citations were part of an effort to pull the wool over his instructor's eyes. (I implied as much in describing them as alibis.) The other group says no, he's simply confused – "clueless" is an adjective I often hear – he's trying to do the right thing, but doesn't know how to go about it. Both assessments are, in fact, plausible, meaning that there can be honest disagreement here. And think what the disagreement is over: we are trying to determine the student's intentions, the very thing that for most people determines how to judge the moral status of a person's actions. In other words, even if we can say without doubt that the student committed plagiarism – in the sense of taking someone else's phrases and ideas – can we really say that he cheated, that he was academically dishonest? If students don't know they're cheating, are they?[6]

How we answer that question will determine what we do with this student. It will, in other words, determine the scope of his future learning.

What Is Learning?

As I said, this exercise is one I use in workshops on academic dishonesty. I tell participants at the outset that my overall message is a simple one: the best strategy for cheating is to ignore it altogether, to pretend it doesn't exist. Before the floodgates of moral indignation open, I quickly steer the discussion to the more easily acceptable point that what we do about cheating will depend on the causes of it. For instance, one cluster of related causes includes peer pressure, the fact that others were doing it, and the lack of an ethical climate. With these causes in mind, I discuss the importance of creating an environment of academic integrity or, more concretely, addressing an honesty policy in the syllabus; of working with students to develop norms of honesty (perhaps by having them vote on whether to use the honor system); and of being a good role model (by, say, scrupulously citing the sources of our lectures). Other causes point to different tactics. Because some cheating results from students perceiving the class, or part of it, to be unfair, I suggest faculty reflect upon whether the demands they make of students are truly reasonable. Where competition and pressure for grades are the cause, one solution is to offer more numerous tests or papers, each counting for a lower share of the final grade. The list goes on, as do the possible remedies. (See the Appendix to this chapter for a brief overview of the causes and remedies of cheating.[7])

In the course of discussing the causes and remedies for cheating, I then turn, via the plagiarism exercise, to the matter of moral ambiguity. My message here is not, as you might have suspected from my title, that because there is no discrete reality of cheating, we can in good conscience ignore it. It does not follow from the existence of a gray area or from epistemic problems identifying examples of cheating that it does not exist or that we need not deal with it. The point I make in workshops is far less dramatic: if we reflect on the long list of things to do with respect to each of the causes of cheating – for example, create an environment of academic integrity, show students that you care about their learning, make reasonable demands – we see that we've created nothing more than a list of good teaching practices. So in the end, I suggest, it isn't about *cheating* so much as it is about *teaching*.[8] My real message, then, is not *really* that we should ignore cheating – I even encourage instructors to report it when they discover it, something that only a minority actually do.[9] It is simply that our focus should be on the much larger picture: good teaching practices. Doing so will allow us to place the ambiguities and complexities of cheating within a useful frame of reference.[10]

In truth, there is more to the story, however. (The chapter title is not mere playfulness.) While I do think that we take care of bad student practices by focusing on good teaching ones, I would also insist that we reconsider the single-mindedness, and at times obsessiveness, with which we wage war on academic dishonesty of any stripe. Part of my concern – a part I also discuss in my workshops – has to do with tone. Issuing daily warnings about the horrors to be released on the poor souls caught in *delicto flagrante*, storming up and down the aisles during tests, casting evil glances at students who so much as breathe in each other's direction – all such actions might extinguish more from students' minds than just thoughts about cheating. Constant vigilance is constant tension, a constant state of distrust that pits educators against educatees. Such an environment might be optimal for a prison camp, but it is unlikely to set a mood conducive to uninhibited inquiry or the open sharing of ideas. As Eble wryly notes, "[t]eaching and learning go better on a nonadversarial basis."[11]

That's part of my concern. The other part – the part I have kept to myself, at least until I write it here – has to do with the more general relationship between dishonesty and learning. Suppose we extend Crews's plagiarism exercise with a fourth student passage, one in which every sentence from Roberts is lifted, reworded, and put back in the same order. One other thing, though: every sentence also has a correct citation identifying Roberts as the source. What do you think – plagiarism or not?

The answer is straightforward. This is not a cheating paper; it is, rather, what we would call a lousy-ass paper. The paper, assuming it goes on like this, has no original insights from the student, and displays only the ability to do some form of advanced transcription of the sort prized in certain varieties of clerical work. (Such a student would have made a good medieval monk, perhaps.) It would certainly be far from clear that this student learned more than either cheater #1 or cheater #2, for, to use Montaigne's colorful metaphor, "spewing up food exactly as you have swallowed it is evidence of a failure to digest and assimilate it, the stomach has not done its job if, during concoction, it fails to change the substance and form of what it is given."[12]

By contrast, consider again my own experiences as a high school student or, to be more precise, as a *cheating* high school student. I described earlier my questionable behavior in history class; let me supplement that jaded episode with another, this one concerning my efforts to promote the literary credentials of my classmates. The class in question was entitled Poetry Workshop, and given its quite minimal requirements it was quite popular with the school's less serious students. As this was the demographic from which came my closest friends, I would receive frequent visits from them. (For reasons that now elude me, I did not myself take the class. Perhaps it conflicted with the aforementioned history class.) Their interest in me was not literary – I was hardly the bard of the school; rather, it stemmed from my owning a record collection that included numerous offerings from obscure artists, many of whom provided their song lyrics on the back cover. Perhaps you can see where this is headed. My friends often came the night before they were to present their work, search my albums for whatever bits of verse they felt might qualify as poetry, and, with perhaps some minimal revisions, write it out. They then merely had to recite "their" doggerel in class the next day without inadvertently hinting at the melodies that no doubt lurked in their minds.

We can make two observations here. First, my friends were cheating and, although I was not actually in the class, so was I: enabling the dishonesty of others is itself an academic infraction. Second, I remained convinced, and my friends often confirmed this to be the case, that the deceit resulted in a fair amount of student learning. To be sure, my ersatz poet friends did little to develop their own original sense of artistic expression, but the weekly task of writing down the lyrics, reciting them aloud, and then having to interpret their meaning to a classroom of often enthusiastic peers – a task that many of them did not anticipate at first, with the humorous result that some were stumped for an interpretation of what was ostensibly their own work – might actually have done more to open their minds to poetry than simply spewing whatever drivel came to their drug-addled minds.

So now let's compare my high school classmates with the author of hypothetical passage number four, by the student who lifted, reworded, and cited correctly every sentence from Roberts. In one camp are students who systematically and premeditatedly cheat; in the other is a student who plays by the rules and learns little or nothing. Can we conclude from these two cases that cheating is acceptable, at least when it promotes learning? I am not suggesting that we can. I do, however, think that we might question whether the relationship between cheating and learning is as straightforward as it might seem. At a minimum, it is far from obvious that the two preclude one another. The only real question is what we should make of that observation.

I have said little about how a craft perspective makes cheating look much different than it does from any other educational perspective. Yes, I have emphasized the need to focus on teaching, not cheating, and although that emphasis is certainly consistent with a craft perspective, it is hardly unique to it. So, in thinking more about the relationship between learning and cheating, we must look further, or perhaps more broadly. Thus far we have examined the dubious ethical practices of students, but what about the practices of those who sit in judgment of them? After all, as every misadventure in research reported in the *Chronicle of Higher Education* demonstrates,[13] dubious ethical practices are clearly not limited to students. Moreover, when we look only at the actions of professors *qua* instructors (not *qua* researchers), the list of possible infractions is not only long, it contains numerous items that clearly affect a class's "ethical environment." To take a fairly mundane and commonplace example, think of two of the questions I raised in the Introduction: can an instructor offer one student a grading arrangement not offered to others, and does accepting one student's excuse – *on faith* – involve inherent unfairness to another? The issue in both cases is fairness, a virtue that, on most accounts, requires instructors to assess students in the same manner and to hold them to the same standards of documentation when it comes to excuses. But what if it could be shown that following the requirements of fairness (so construed) actively discouraged student learning? What then?

Think about the following hypothetical situation, one most professors have encountered repeatedly in their careers. A student comes to your office with a paper for which you have given him a C. On that paper are your copious comments pointing to its virtues and the areas in which there was room for improvement. It turns out that your comments were effective: the student, far from being discouraged by the C, is champing at the bit to make revisions and produce the work that will give him both confidence and pride – one that, in other words, will add greatly to his learning (and, he hopes, to his grade). Your inclination – if you think only of his learning – is to say, "Go ahead, I can't wait to see what you come up with." The problem, however, is that you've made no mention of a rewrite policy to the class, and thus in responding this way, you would be treating him differently than the others. It would involve unfairness. Knowing *this* fact, you deny his request and send him on his way.

Did you do the right thing? In answering, let's begin by questioning the manner in which we have construed fairness. Our standard intuition seems to be that students should receive equal treatment. But is that really the case? And if so, what do we mean by equal treatment? We certainly don't treat students equally when it comes to the grades we assign them. Nor do we treat them equally in our expectations – in class discussions, for example, we often push some students further than others. Both examples point to the fact that equal treatment depends upon the characteristic we're looking at: as Aristotle famously pointed out, "equality consists in treating equals equally and unequals unequally."[14] Although it is true that students *qua* students are not morally deserving of the same grade, they are *with respect to the work they do*: all students who do C-level work deserve to receive a C. Likewise, differences in the way we treat them in class – grilling some more deeply than others, for instance – merely reflects our desire to treat them equally with respect to that aspect of students that really matters: their capacity to grasp the material. Assuming we want all students to learn as much as they – individually – can learn, equal treatment in this regard certainly would not mandate (ethically, at least) identical pedagogical strategies.

With this thought, we have reconstrued fairness such that we might now say the following: an instructor who ignores differences among students that are relevant to their capacity to learn – by, say, offering them all identical instruction – is violating the norms of fairness. Such an action still could be considered fair on other grounds; the only question is whether the relevant fact about students that the instructor is considering– their capacity to learn – is the fact about them that the instructor needs to consider above all others. If it is – if student learning is what it's all about – then fairness can be construed as doing what it takes, within the limits of our time and energy (about which, more below), to make every student learn as much as possible. If one student needs more time than another to get the same out of a test or paper, fairness dictates that we give that student more time. And the same would hold true of our hypothetical student seeking a rewrite. We recognize this principle of fairness in our desire to accommodate students with disabilities; here we simply extend the argument to any and all differences in learning capacity that students present. Seen in this light, there is no contradiction between the mandates of fairness and those of student learning; indeed the former is derived with respect to the latter. If our students are learning equally, and if their learning is truly our goal, then whatever unequal treatment we might have given them is ethically justified (because it is pedagogically justified). I certainly can conceive of a situation where I would not lose a wink of sleep over a decision to grant an extension to one – and *only* one – student. If I go to hell for it, I'll at least have in my company a fair number of good educators.

Now perhaps you object that I never should have gotten myself into such a situation in the first place, that I should have had policies in place to deal with such contingencies. My reply is simply that we need to be realistic: we cannot plan for everything, and even if we could, the "right" policies easily could require far more work than any of us is either capable of or wishes to do. In fact I suspect that a more common objection to a rewrite request is rooted less in ethical or pedagogical considerations than in the quite understandable desire to limit one's workload. I am certainly guilty of harboring this desire, and see no reason we should deny it to ourselves[15] – survival, after all, is a good thing, and teaching as a craft is certainly not without its survival moments.

We are left, then, with an imperfect world, one filled with choices that admit of no clear moral or pedagogical boundaries, and where decisions often need to be made in less time than anyone has. In the heat of extemporaneous deliberations, the skill of improvisation looms large. At the root of that skill lies a willingness to look at our own role in whatever predicament the student is in, and also an openness to questioning our most basic assumptions: is it true that learning must take a back seat to fairness? and what *is* fairness?

We should see now how the inclusion of teachers' actions changes our perspective on cheating. Most obviously it reminds us that teachers and their actions are a part of the environment. There are really two subtle points here: first, there is an environment; second, there are individuals whose job it is to try to shape it. What the first point indicates is that, whatever else it is, cheating is never an isolated act. Rather, it is one that is affected by the situations in which individuals find themselves. Thus, to get to the second point, professors, as the architects of those situations, bear some responsibility for it. The practical conclusion to draw here is that, as Lang puts it, "if you want people to cheat or not cheat on a task ... *you modify the environment in which they are completing the task.*"[16] In a sense, then, our moral approbation is better directed at cheating *environments* than at the individuals within them. Or, to be more contentious, we might even say that, from the professor's perspective, the responsibility is *entirely* hers. Why, to pick up a theme central to craft teaching, should we dwell on student responsibility (except in thinking about how to affect their behavior) when there is so much to think about with respect to the things *we* can do?

It might be helpful, in fleshing out this perspective, to return to the plagiarism exercise with which I began this chapter. This time, however, let's adjust the scenario a bit. Imagine that the exercise looks exactly the same, but that now we are given the following background information:

1. The course was a freshman level introduction to history.
2. The assignment contained a statement that read "students should hand in only their own work and should not plagiarize the work of others." This statement was the assignment's only mention of plagiarism.
3. The course syllabus contained a statement that read "Violation of the academic dishonesty rules is grounds for receiving an 'F' in the course; see the University Policy on Academic Honesty for further information." Beyond this statement, no mention was made in class or in writing of academic dishonesty (other than the statement mentioned in #2).
4. 100 percent of the course grade was based on the assignment.
5. 20 percent of the class was found to have plagiarized.

6. Among the students who received a grade, the class average was
   a D+.
7. On student evaluations given at the end of the course, the average
   score on the item "The professor motivated me to do the work" was
   a 2.1 on a five-point Likert scale, where 1 = disagree strongly;
   5 = agree strongly.

With this information in mind, let us return to the two students who,
we determined, plagiarized from the source material, and let us agree
that none of these background conditions changes this fact. The issue
we want to examine is whether these conditions have any bearing on
the issue. I am not asking the direct and simple "should these factors
affect how the cheaters are treated?" My interest is in the larger issue of
where the cheating fits within the context that these conditions partially
describe.

Consider the first four conditions. Each one alters the learning environment in a manner that makes cheating more likely. We have young
students, many of whom perhaps have had little or no exposure to norms
of academic honesty; they are in a class that provides little guidance on
the issue and only rare mention of it; and they are confronted with an
assignment that offers the highest stakes – and thus the highest degree
of stress – possible. This perfect storm of conditions makes the next one
unsurprising, unless we reflect that 20 percent is on the low side of what
we might expect. It also goes a long way toward explaining the final two
conditions, both of which are symptoms of an environment where we
might expect to see cheating. The class average suggests that students
were not fully aware of the professor's expectations and – we might infer
– therefore lacked confidence ("self-mastery") that they could succeed.
Couple that fact with a lack motivation and, well, bad things are going
to happen.

So, for how much of this perfect storm is the professor of this class
responsible? In a certain sense, he is responsible for all of it – although
the first condition was simply a fact to which one must respond.

Conditions two through four stem from policies for which the professor is solely responsible. The fact that these policies were in place for an introductory course (condition one) makes them all the less excusable. Conditions five through seven point to facts about the course for which the professor clearly played a part. We could speculate about how large a part, or what other factors also might have played a role, but what's the point? The extent to which those causes involved factors beyond the professor's control is precisely the extent to which they should be ignored. The point, then, is not that cheating students are without responsibility; rather, it is that whatever responsibility they have must be seen in light of the professor's *prior* responsibility for creating the context in which the cheating occurred.

Think, for example, of decisions that all instructors make in creating courses.[17] Some decisions address honesty directly: what will my syllabus say about academic integrity? what will *I* say? what format will my tests and paper assignments have (assignments vary greatly in their "cheat-ability")? Other decisions address honesty indirectly: how many tests/assignments will I have? for what percentage of the total will each count (lowering the stakes of any particular assignment will reduce cheating)? how will I learn the students' names (learning their names will reduce cheating)? how will I promote students' intrinsic motivation to learn or instill in them high expectations of success? how will I get students to think with a "mastery" rather than a "performance" orientation?[18] Note that, although these questions are about what the *professor* will do, we ask them only because they're relevant to what *students* will do.

To illustrate the point further, let's add another condition:

8. Students were given the assignment the night before the due date.

At this point the situation becomes truly absurd, so it is not surprising that it points to an equally absurd conclusion – namely, that the actions of students #1 and #2 from the plagiarism test constitute a quite reasonable response to the kind of teaching that lacks any real concern for learning.[19] Under the circumstances, it is difficult even to call what they have done cheating. Is it cheating to seek a way around a set of extraordinarily poor teaching techniques – techniques that create environments where any desire students might have to learn is frustrated at every turn? If ever a situation illustrated just how closely intertwined the ethics of student behavior and the ethics of faculty behavior are, this one surely does. And make no mistake: professors who teach with obvious disregard for, or ignorance about, such basic educational principles are acting unethically – so much so that it is not unreasonable to ask, in this situation, who is cheating whom?

The key point is that cheaters are players in a drama that is directed by us, and because we play a vital part in creating the drama in which they play a role, we play a vital part in creating *them* (the cheaters). I don't mean to deny their agency; I mean only to place it, as we must with any claims of agency, in its proper context – one in which our roles are clearly implicated.[20]

To add to the absurdity, now let us add one final condition:

9. The course is at an institution with a zero-tolerance policy in which any academic honesty offense is grounds for immediate dismissal.

In thinking about this last condition, let's begin by admitting that, as an abstract principle, the policy is not without merit. We can certainly imagine justifications that draw on utilitarian or retributive logic. And if those justifications considered the true scope of the matter, perhaps the discussion could end there. What would we say, however, to Lang's argument that "the best reason we have for *not* instituting hard and uniform punishments for the first-time offenders ... is that such responses do a terrible job of helping students learn"?[21] Surely the point is salient: utilitarian, retributive, or other arguments make sense only to the degree they keep this broader context in mind. And to the reply that, in addition to learning history or math, students must also learn right from wrong, Lang points out that zero-tolerance policies also might teach them "that the institution values rules over learning, or that it affords students no second chances, or that the institution's faculty operate as if they were on a battlefield, hell-bent on catching and punishing cheaters, instead of providing a learning environment in which all constituents are working together to help students learn."[22]

What we need to accept here is not an argument against a zero-tolerance policy, but the larger point that Lang so clearly demonstrates: *any* response to – or policy directed toward – cheating will have effects well beyond those we initially considered and, in light of that fact, *all* responses, to the extent we take seriously the task at hand, involve massively complex considerations. In light of *this* observation, the only general statement we can make is that *no* response to this, or *any*, cheating situation is straightforward or obvious.[23]

As one last bit of evidence for this thought, consider an alternative to the final condition:

9. The course is at an institution with a student-run honor code. Students sign an oath to abide by standards of academic honesty and are responsible for policing themselves. Faculty are not present during tests and exams, and all cases of alleged dishonesty are brought before an all-student disciplinary board that decides on guilt or innocence and, in the former cases, the penalty.

Here let me admit not just that I think this policy has merit, but that I have personally pushed for it at my own institution. My defense is along the following lines: the problem with most academic honesty policies is that they do not let students learn perhaps the most important lesson of all: *it's up to you.* Educators can tell students not to cheat, and punish them if they do, but even if we stopped all cheating activities, we would not have thereby encouraged the type of learning that truly matters. If students refrained from cheating because we placed video cameras in the classroom and ran their papers through cheating software, what, precisely, would we have stopped? Certainly not the desire to cheat. As such, could we really say that students who, out of fear of the consequences, did not cheat had thereby learned in an ethical manner? And if our understanding of learning was sufficiently capacious to capture its moral aspects, would we say that they had learned, *period*? Not cheating under such conditions might be prudent behavior, perhaps, but in that regard it would differ little from cheating under more lax conditions. So what *really* is the concern for which we design our honesty policies: to stop discrete instances of cheating or to wean students from the disposition to do it? What, after all, would we think about an institution of higher learning that simply churned out individuals who *knew things* – about history, about literature, about physics, even about learning itself – but whose maturity, moral development, and character had been untouched by the experience? Would we say they *really* knew things, at least in a complete sense?

For those disposed to a broad view of learning, one that encompasses character as well as intellect and creativity,[24] it is perhaps easy to see the virtue of placing the whole academic honesty enterprise squarely in the laps of students, telling them when they arrive at our institutions: "You will find ways to cheat, cut corners, and so on. If such behavior is attractive to you, you should take it as a sign that you do not truly understand why you are here and, worse, that you have some moral maturing to do. We will not get in your way. Our doing so would not change the fact that you thought cheating was the right thing to do, and that fact is all that really matters. Know that we, your instructors, would think the worse of you were we to know what you had done. And know also that, were you honest at least with yourselves, you would think the worse of those selves." The emphasis here is not on the self-defeating nature of cheating – on the fact that we cheat only ourselves; as I have pointed out, I'm not sure that statement is even true, as cheating and learning of some sort might go hand in hand. Rather, the emphasis here is on learning, but only of a certain sort – the sort that occurs when we no longer need to be punished for doing what we know to be wrong.

As I have made this very argument in the past, I obviously think there's much to be said for it, at least in principle.[25] Clearly, though, there might be practical issues to consider. I would concede, for example, that such a policy would not be appropriate for *every* institution. In fact, I would say that, at many institutions, the learning environment is not right for it, or at least not ready for it, and so implementing it would lead to disaster. Where such policies do exist,[26] they are successful to the extent they are accompanied by a particular type of community ethos, one that requires several conditions to be in place. Simply to impose a student-run honor code on *any* set of conditions, including those with none of the social mores that such codes are designed to create, is to miss the larger point about academic integrity: it is the product of an overwhelming number of variables, most of which exist well beyond the classrooms in which certain individuals toil valiantly to game the system. Thus a policy that places cheating in the laps of students paradoxically makes what educators do in creating a learning (and thus non-cheating) environment *more*, not less, important.

Down the Rabbit Hole

By now, I imagine that all this talk of complexity has tried your patience. We began with a simple look at an individual act, only to discover that whatever simplicity there was to that act was merely an illusion. (Was it plagiarism? Was it intentional?) From there, things only got worse, as concern for a cheating student gave way to concern about a cheating environment, giving us innumerably more variables to consider. And to the extent that individual students remained in our sights, we were then confronted with the issue of whether cheating was an *act* or a *disposition*, and thus whether our concern was with what students *do* or with the far larger matter of *who they are*.

In short I have only scratched the surface of the factors involved in sorting out cheating, and yet already all hope of definitive answers appears lost. Moreover I have thus far avoided factors that we prefer not to acknowledge. For example, consider what might happen if, after knowingly nodding our heads in disapproval that a student has dared to violate norms of scholarly behavior that we hold as sacred (in theory at least), we were to take a long look in the mirror and ask if we really have the time, energy, or interest always to be concerned with the pursuit of justice – especially where the pursuit of justice might bring a backlash in the student evaluations that play such an inordinate role in promotion and tenure decisions. In short, even after we decide what our responsibilities are with respect to cheating, we need to place them in the context of the actual and, at times, quite stressful pace of higher education. As I emphasized above with respect to offering rewrites, we can be responsible for doing only what we can *reasonably* do, and in some contexts turning a blind eye to an egregious act of cheating might be *just* the thing to do.

So it's complicated – very complicated. And, as I've tried to make clear, *that is the point.* Let me drive it home more forcefully. It's not just that there are seemingly endless factors to consider; it's that, to get a handle on any situation, we must look not at all of these trees but at the forest they collectively create. Little is gained in the broader scheme of things by focusing on the narrow scope of them, and so we must begin by asking about the whole – what is the essence of the learning experience? – and then examine how all the pieces that comprise the whole affect one another and fit (or not) together.

Of course, to make matters worse, there are many different wholes, each at a different level of the learning experience. The most familiar whole is a course: one that has a teacher, students, a subject, assignments, readings, in-class activities, homework, methods of assessment, desired learning goals. (I could go on.) Within a course, we have a particular class on any given day, one that has *its* own components. And courses themselves are within larger wholes: departments, with their rules, curricula, and requirements; universities with theirs; political entities and accrediting bodies with theirs.

Cheating, too, has components relative to each level. For example, a test on a certain day has a seating arrangement, counts for a certain share of the final grade, comes at a certain point in the semester, and deals with material of a certain nature – all factors that play a part in determining whether cheating occurs. Similarly a course has a stated academic honesty policy, is or is not a requirement, has or does not have clearly stated requirements – again, all factors that play a role in how honestly students approach their learning. As we go to broader levels, we find factors unique to each: departments have stated policies, universities have climates of academic integrity, professions have standards, nations have cultural mores – once again, factors that play a role in the level of honesty. We might even say that floating above all such levels – or perhaps submerged at their foundations – are the conceptions of knowledge and standards of understanding that inform and define them all.[27]

There are, then, two ways to look at an issue such as cheating. One way is to see what its qualities are at various levels – what the components of cheating are at the level of the course, the department, or the university. The task here is to get a sense of how cheating plays a role at each level, and thus gain a better idea of why it exists at any one of them. The problem with this perspective is that it involves a far larger purview than most instructors have – or have time to have. It is enough to think about cheating in the context of the courses we offer; its larger institutional elements are, for most of us, someone else's headache.

For this reason the second way to look at cheating is quite enough, and in a sense it isn't really looking at cheating. Here we focus not on cheating as it plays out at many different levels, but on all the many aspects (cheating among them) of *one* level. If – as it will most commonly be for teachers – that environment is the course, then we see cheating as something that affects and is affected by the other components of the whole. The key to this perspective lies with its point of reference: instead of examining an aspect of education such as cheating in isolation from other aspects (as the first perspective would) or even as part of an ensemble of discrete, but related facts (cheating as a product of individual moral failing, an unsound method of assessment, an overly harsh institutional policy), the starting point and, more important, the *destination* are always the whole: the learning experience in its totality. The task is to keep in mind not merely the wide variety of contexts in which learning occurs, but, rather, the whole.

Now that statement is somewhat bewildering, so let me put it in the context of cheating. From the perspective I am suggesting, cheating ceases to be a discrete act – *this* student committing *this* act for *this* class – but is, rather, simultaneously a matter of testing and lecturing and grading and constructing syllabi and all the other myriad aspects of a learning environment, just as all of those aspects are always, in some sense, matters of cheating. As such, cheating is a *symptom* (a key word) of a dysfunctional educational experience, one that in some way is in a state of imbalance. In coping with it, we keep a constant eye on the experience as a whole, asking whether its constituent parts are in their proper relationship, with "proper" defined as that which creates a balanced whole. And what constitutes "balanced"? A balanced educational experience is one that achieves the end for which it is designed. In my craft understanding, it is one that gives students the desire to learn – to teach themselves. Those experiences can be balanced in numerous ways with numerous different proportions of components, and so we need to worry less about any one approach to cheating or testing or grading, and more about finding approaches to all of those components that somehow work together to achieve the balance that creates eager and inquisitive students.

On this view, problems such as cheating have no independent existence – they are, to use a philosophical term, *epiphenomena* – and their solutions can be judged only by their effect on the whole. We do well to know the *tendencies* of various educational policies and methods – what effects they tend to produce – but we need to bear in mind the difference between a tendency and an iron-clad law. Such an argument is hardly music to the ears of those in search of *a priori* rules and simple algorithms. It is unsettling to hear that policies and rules have *tendencies*, rather than definitive *consequences*, and that tasks such as handling student dishonesty are not mere child's play. So be it. Such – as I underscore in the final chapter – is the nature of an endeavor that is, above all else, *a craft*.

With this larger perspective in mind – larger, that is, than one focused only on cheating – what in the end should we think about the pedagogical ploy, perhaps used by my high school history teacher, of promoting learning by luring students into cheating? Might it be acceptable for faculty to ignore – encourage even – cheating in cases where it results in learning?[28] And what of our broader concern about the relationship between learning and cheating? Is it inverse? Proportionate? *Is* there a relationship?

As I hope I have made clear, from a craft perspective there can be no definitive answers to such questions. To be sure, all things considered equal, ethical practices are better than unethical ones, and, in any case, there are certainly limits to the use of unethical means. Poisoning a medical student to provide her classmates with a first-hand look at the resultant death throes would certainly remove unwanted abstraction from a lesson on toxins, but the price of the ploy would be too high, especially if the student were a good one. If we bear such limits in mind, however, there might be good reasons to stop short of categorical ethical stands. Even if we agreed – and I do – that unethical behavior constitutes a breakdown in the learning process, I still think we could conceive of learning environments in which the breakdown was an acceptable price to pay – where it helped to make the environment preferable to any readily available alternatives. Such moral ambiguity is troubling, no doubt, but only to the extent that we kid ourselves into believing that an activity involving so many interpersonal dynamics could somehow lend itself to straightforward and obvious moral imperatives.

Appendix:
Cheating – Causes and Remedies

To compensate for the somewhat abstract concerns of this chapter, I close with a few practical considerations to bear in mind.

Reasons students cheat:

- recognition that others are doing it;
- perception that professor seems not to care (about cheating or about student learning);
- peer pressure;
- lack of an ethical climate;
- competition and pressure for grades;
- perceived unfairness;
- ignorance of what constitutes cheating.

What teachers can do to minimize it:

1. Create an environment of academic integrity:
   - address your honesty policy in the syllabus;
   - develop norms of honesty – have them vote on whether to use an honor system;
   - model academic integrity;
   - address it when it occurs; remember that ignoring cheating tends to encourage it, both in your class *and* in your colleagues' classes;
     - report the matter to your department head;
     - read and follow your campus's stated procedures on academic dishonesty;
     - gather evidence.

2. Show students you care about cheating *and* about their learning:
   - talk to students who aren't doing well; students are less likely to cheat if they aren't anonymous faces in the crowd;
   - be vigilant during tests, but be wary that you aren't perceived as an untrusting cop;
   - learn their names.

3. Make *reasonable* demands.

4. Increase the number of graded assignments to diminish the pressure surrounding any one of them.

5. Call or email your campus's teaching center.

6. Explain to students what honest intellectual inquiry *is*.

7. *Most important*: promote student learning!

Concluding Thoughts

Teaching Moment 5. A few years ago I found myself barreling down I-85 between Atlanta and Athens, Georgia, with a three-ring binder of lecture notes wedged between my lap and the steering wheel. As I rehearsed the lecture I was about to give, I had a couple of concerns. For one the angle on the notes wasn't quite right, and although I managed to improve on it by propping the binder up higher so it jammed tight between my stomach and the middle of the wheel, the adjustment wasn't perfect. The regular honking of the horn that came with every exhale didn't really bother me that much, but it sure did seem to tick off some of the adjacent drivers. (Out of consideration, I started holding my breath for long periods of time, although the resultant dizziness made me swerve a bit.) The other concern was with steering, but thankfully Athens is a fairly straight shot from Atlanta.

So what brought about this curious state of affairs? Although I certainly had not planned on a sixteen-lane review session, all hope of an early departure had been dashed by extended meetings and last-minute student emails. By the time I set off for Athens, I had an hour and a half to get to my lecture, coincidently the same amount of time MapQuest had predicted it would take. The sudden realization that MapQuest hadn't factored in other matters – fighting traffic, road-rage banter, parking, walking from the car – brought home just how much the perception of lateness depends on which side of the podium you expect to find yourself.

Fortunately MapQuest grossly underestimated the speed at which late academics can travel. Not only did I make it roughly on time, I managed, in addition to giving my notes a final review, to mull over a topic that had concerned me for much of the week: lecturing. A few days before, I had led a faculty discussion on the topic, and since then I had kept coming back to the variety of techniques discussed in the literature – techniques with which many of my colleagues had dabbled. The whole matter is somewhat idiosyncratic, especially when it comes to the notes people use. Some people have copious notes, others none at all. Some use PowerPoint slides as their notes. Some have a full script that, to varying degrees, they read.

It was this latter technique that had grabbed much of my attention, mostly because, well, I confess I often use it myself. I say *confess* because the academic literature on notes is unanimous in its disdain for word-for-word scripts. Often the disdain comes with bold, italicized lettering: *DO NOT write your notes out word for word!* To my thinking, any practice that elicits such universal condemnation cannot be all bad, and so I had been thinking about which of its untold virtues educational experts would find so threatening. I started by wondering why I used it, and my first thought was that, frankly, at times I *need* a script. The problem is with my memory, which, especially when I'm standing in front of more than four people, is pretty short. *Really* short: non-existent, actually. Sometimes when I get to the predicate of a sentence, it's anyone's guess what the subject was. Given this sad state of affairs, if I want to say something in just a certain way, I need to write it down to make sure that twenty-four hours later I still have access to it.

Now I should quickly note that I rarely lecture to a class for more than about fifteen minutes at a time, and I do so only when I'm aiming at the more basic levels of knowledge. Moreover the particular wording I wish to preserve is not standard academic prose; it's something more conversational. In crafting it I just start speaking in a friendly mode, as if I were trying to explain the idea to someone in front of me. I often channel a particular student, usually one whom I know might have particular difficulty with the topic. Maybe he's the one who's more concerned with the pizza he's eating than the lecture I'm giving (no doubt because he's stoned); or perhaps he's the one who asks questions the bizarreness of which threaten the very fabric of space-time. (Indeed, he might be stoned as well.) Sometimes I just channel my former undergraduate self, who, coincidently enough, was a sort of 1970s amalgamation of the two students just mentioned. Anyway, once I have a student in my head, I just start to talk to him or her, writing down the things I say. The next day I might or might not say it just as I've written it – often I find a better way – but in any case the script is there if I need it, and, given that it doesn't conform to the norms of academic writing, I'm reasonably sure that students have no idea it's all written down.

I would argue that this technique promotes the type of clarity that comes only when we put our thoughts to paper. It also has the virtue of making notes that will still have some meaning in two, five, or ten years – whenever they are next needed. (And for some reason its continuing meaning invariably leads to extensive revisions, resulting in notes that are perennially new.) Of course, in terms of presentation, a lot depends on where my eyes are when I deliver the words. If they're buried deep in the podium, then what I say surely will be *presumed* to be written (why else would I have my head down?). As such, it likely will lead to the same level of attention that is accorded flight attendants as they explain the intricacies of the seatbelt before takeoff. So my eyes need to be up, looking at the students I am talking to, much as we do normally when we're talking to people.

But here is where my memory problems come in: I *need* the script, at least at times. Yet now it turns out I can't really be looking at it. So what to do? My solution has always been to prepare it in a certain way. First, the words have to be in a huge font – 16 points at a minimum. Second, I make certain keywords bold enough to stand out, even at a glance. Third, I write only a phrase or two on every line, so it looks like poetry. Little tricks like these give me a fighting chance of keeping my head up long enough to pull off the ruse – which, in virtue of writing this, might have just gotten a lot harder.

It was the difficulty of this ruse that I had in mind on that trip to Athens. In fact, halfway there I realized I had stumbled upon a fairly useful training exercise. The problem in the classroom is that nothing very bad happens if you bury your head in your notes. And what bad things *do* happen – your students fall asleep; they start talking to one another; they get up and leave – you aren't really aware of anyway because, as I said, your head is buried in your notes. In fact, if you're into wholesale self-delusion, you might even imagine that your students are all listening with rapt attention, in which case there's a *dis*incentive to picking your head up, as doing so would only shatter your dreams. All in all, then, keeping your head down in class comes with no dire consequences (of which you are aware).

Not so if you're at the wheel of a car going 75 mph on the Interstate to Athens, Georgia. The stakes are much, *much* higher here. Keep your head down too long and bang! – lecture's over (although, again, you might not be aware of that fact). To be honest the experience was pretty fun; exhilarating even. By the time I reached Athens, I was convinced that my in-car lecture was not only a great training technique, it could also serve as a skill-testing requirement: if you can give a lecture to your department chair over your cell phone as you commute to work on a major Interstate, and you succeed in *getting* to work, then you've earned the right to teach your class. For safety's sake, you'd want to use the hands-free phone, of course, although if you wanted an added degree of difficulty, you could keep the phone in your hand. Hell, you could even throw a Happy Meal into the mix.[1]

If I seem to have gone from defending the virtues of a vilified pedagogical practice to suggesting it as a required skill, then I might have gone too far. My intention was emphatically not to suggest the universal adoption of any one lecturing technique but precisely the opposite: given the challenges of university teaching, we should not be quick to discard *any* one tool in the pedagogical toolbox. Even the most vilified practices can sometimes offer us just the right inroad into an effective learning environment, just as the most universally revered might, in some contexts, occlude even a glimmer of it. The universal truth here is that there *is* no universal truth here. The success of whatever practices we adopt will be determined by their fit with a particular situation at a particular point in time.

Which brings me back to cheating ...

It might seem odd to end a book on teaching as a craft with a chapter on a notorious breakdown of the learning environment. Yet perhaps it makes sense: it often takes pathology to reveal the essence and nature of things, and in this regard cheating offers the clearest possible illustration of just how involved this craft really is. Teachers do not just prepare classes, assess students' work, lead discussions, and handle the variety of disciplinary and interpersonal problems that arise. They do *all* those things – *together*. The craft of teaching arises in seeing how these many activities interlock, and how none of them stands apart from the whole in which they are embedded. We can talk about the best way to lecture or the proper use of technology or effective strategies to prevent cheating, but none of our answers can be *the* answer, for the simple reason that none of the dilemmas we face is repeatable – all are unique. The craft of teaching, then, cannot be reduced to the individual skills involved in bringing to others the joy of learning. It is, rather, the use of all of those skills simultaneously, in just the right degree and at just the right time. It is juggling – but where each ball can change shape, size, and weight at any moment, and where, in the effort to keep some aloft, others might hit the floor.

Perhaps that makes teaching seem a bit pointless: if you can never get it completely right – or worse, if there *is* no "completely right" – why bother? My response is that the acceptance of impossible complexity need not be an admission of defeat. I, at least, don't take it that way, even though the more I reflect on my own teaching, the less sure I am about it. From my perspective, accepting the complexity of teaching affirms that the doubts I have are doubts that I *should* have; it gives voice to my reassuring suspicion that the career I have chosen is not an easy undertaking – for *anyone*. If it is a noble career, as people are fond of saying, it is so not simply because it can do so much that is good, but also because it demands so much of "ye who enter here." The key is not, as Dante suggests just before these words, to abandon all hope. To the contrary, that response is appropriate only where teaching is approached as a simple matter, one devoid of the endless variety, constant tensions, and, at times, seemingly insurmountable challenges that serve as the hallmarks of a craft. Those who approach teaching in this way (*algorithmically* perhaps) emphatically are not engaged in a craft.[2]

Far from being dispirited, then, we should find comfort in the knowledge that many teaching problems, such as cheating, admit of no objectively right response and that *all* responses are only parts of a puzzle, each with a limited, although potentially quite salutary, effect on the whole. Accepting this fact allows us to judge those responses in a meaningful context, one freed from delusions of being able to solve all problems with a confident stroke of some pedagogical wand. There might be too many ways to think about all the situations that confront us daily, but that simply means that, in teaching, unlike in juggling, there are only *degrees* of success. None of us is expected to keep all the balls in the air all the time or even to keep most in the air most of the time. There are simply too many variables for that expectation to constitute a reasonable goal.

A better analogy is to chess, a game in which there are more possible moves than atoms in the universe. The beauty of chess is that, even with the effectively limitless nature of possibilities and the quite limited nature of the cognitive capacity we bring to them, we can still play. We can come up with answers. They might not always be the most effective answers, nor will they always be the most beautiful ones – the ones that merited praise as much for *how* they brought about a desired effect as for their bringing it about. There is, however, something better than either the most effective or the most elegant answer: there is *our* answer, the answer that reflects on us as teachers. This answer is not better in some objective sense of the word; it is better because it stems from a creative process that is unique to us, one that is emblazoned with our own idiosyncratic personalities. This aspect of teaching reflects its true nature as both a calling and a craft. It reflects the fact that, like the learning it is intended to create, teaching is more about searching for the right answers than it is about finding *any* of them.

Here my thoughts return to what I said in Chapter One about a craft – namely, that it must be a conscious, intentional activity – an activity of which we are always aware and on which we always reflect. We cannot, as the leitmotif of our commercial culture would have us believe, *Just do it*.[3] We need to do it deliberately, with purpose, and not merely because that's the path to successful practice, but because, to be a craft, these practices must embody *our* conscious efforts, rather than the myriad imperatives that confront us. To reflect, then, is vital, for in giving us a steady view of what we are capable of producing, our inward gaze keeps us in touch with the true object of our craft: ourselves.[4]

Recall how our view of cheating students shifted from what they *do* to the far larger matter of *who they are*. On such a view we see their lives not just as discrete moments, but as embodiments of character, of personality, of capacities, and of shortcomings – aspects that do not emerge without some movement through time. A similar shift occurs when we view teaching through a craft lens, a point that brings us back to "the moments" with which I began this book. I argued there that the moments we experience constitute the essence of all that education is about. My concern was that we not lose sight of those moments in a vain attempt to capture larger and general "truths." In closing, however, I need to sharpen that view and suggest that, although these moments indeed have their own intrinsic worth, in one respect (the craft respect) their significance lies in what they reveal to us as they blur and run together over time, as they form a picture of what we do and who we are – a picture that is continually changing and that emphatically cannot be reduced to single moments. About ourselves, then, we *can* generalize, not in the academic way I dismissed before, but merely in the way that all thoughtful people – all practitioners of a craft – must.

In this sense we serve two masters, one for whom the moments are all that matter – "all roads lead to the classroom" – and the other for whom "what matters" cannot possibly be understood apart from who we are as teachers and why we find ourselves in the classroom in the first place. If this dialectical tension makes you uncomfortable, recall how easily we live with it in other walks of life. When we learn to play a game or a musical instrument, or when we take up a skilled hobby or an artistic endeavor, we do so to experience the momentary joys such pursuits offer. But we also have no difficulty seeing, and gaining satisfaction from, our slow development over time as chess or guitar players, bird watchers or jewelry makers. The particular and the general – the moments and their passage – are, here, *both* necessary to us, as neither makes sense in the absence of the other. The fact that development is slow reflects the difficulty of any one moment. That there *is* development – that, in the course of changing others, we change ourselves – offers us the best reason we could possibly have to stay with it. Put otherwise: we do what we do both for the occasional joy it brings and because doing what we do makes us people for whom that occasional joy still matters.

Notes

Notes to the Preface

1 In an effort to avoid the somewhat cumbersome he/she and him/her, I use both male and female pronouns randomly throughout the book.
2 For an argument that teaching deserves the same degree of recognition as research, see Ernest L. Boyer, *Scholarship Reconsidered: Priorities of the Professoriate* (San Francisco: Jossey-Bass, 1997).
3 The reference here is to Don Finkel's wonderful *Teaching with Your Mouth Shut* (Portsmouth, NH: Boynton/Cook, 2000).

Notes to Introduction

1 Rousseau, in describing parents proudly displaying their precocious child, gives an early (pre-Palin) account of the technique: "At table they did not fail, according to the French method, to make the little gentleman babble a great deal. The vivacity natural to his age, along with the expectation of certain applause, made him reel off countless stupidities, in the midst of which from time to time there came a few lucky words which caused the rest to be forgotten." Jean-Jacques Rousseau, *Emile: Or, On Education*, ed. and trans. Allen Bloom (New York: Basic Books, 1979), 110.
2 The student's name, by the way, was Jason Jenson. I told him a few years later that I had read his paper at a few conferences when lecturing on grading, but that I always protected his identity. He responded by saying that, no, he wanted full recognition. I can't say I blame him.
3 The technique, as I later found out, has been around for a while – in fact, a long while. In 1962 Gruber and Weitman demonstrated in far more scientific fashion than I just did how effective teacherless classrooms can be. See Leslie R. Beach, "Self-Directed Student Groups and College Learning," *Higher Education* 3, no. 2 (1974): 187–200.

4 Jack Grove, "The Best Student Excuses," *Inside Higher Ed*, 30 August 2012, available online at http://www.insidehighered.com/news/2012/08/30/british-lecturer-compiles-best-student-excuses.

5 T.S. Eliot suggests otherwise, although I take his thoughts to be directed more at producers than consumers of literature: "No poet, no artist of any art, has his complete meaning alone. His significance, his appreciation is the appreciation of his relation to the dead poets and artists. You cannot value him alone; you must set him, for contrast and comparison, among the dead. I mean this as a principle of aesthetic, not merely historical, criticism." T.S. Eliot, "Tradition and the Individual Talent," *Poetry Foundation*, 13 October 2009, available online at http://www.poetryfoundation.org/learning/essay/237868?page=1, accessed 13 December 2013. I have no doubt that criticism can illuminate meaning and, as such, can contribute to our appreciation of a work. I would only question whether such a change in appreciation always occurs at an aesthetic level.

6 The idea was Sarahbeth Gehl's.

7 Robert B. Barr and John Tagg, "From Teaching to Learning – A New Paradigm for Undergraduate Education," *Change: The Magazine of Higher Learning* 27, no. 6 (1995): 12.

8 "[A]s you and your colleagues begin to speak the new language, you will then also begin to think and act out of the new paradigm" (ibid., 25).

9 Barr and Tagg suggest that, because of the instructional paradigm, "colleges create 'complex structures to provide for the activity of teaching conceived primarily as delivering 50-minute lectures" (ibid., 13); "student outcomes are simply irrelevant to the successful functioning and funding of a college" (16); and that "the teacher's job is to 'cover the material' as outlined in the disciplinary syllabus" (19–20). They continue: it "wastes not only institutional resources but the time and energy of students. We waste our students' time with registration lines, bookstore lines, lock-step class scheduling, and redundant courses and requirements" (23); and "faculty are conceived primarily as disciplinary experts who impart knowledge by lecturing. They are the essential feature of the 'instructional delivery system'" (24). Correspondingly, the learning paradigm "ends the lecture's privileged position, honoring in its place whatever approaches serve best to prompt learning of particular knowledge by particular students" (14). It means that "a college takes responsibility for the aggregate of student learning and success [and for] for each individual student's learning" (15); and that it "conceives of faculty as primarily the designers of learning environments; they study and apply best methods for producing learning and student success" (24).

10 For a good discussion of this issue, see Andrew Hacker and Claudia Dreifus, "Who's minding the schools?" *New York Times*, 8 June 2013, available online at http://www.nytimes.com/2013/06/09/opinion/sunday/the-common-core-whos-minding-the-schools.html. Diana Ravitch is also a compelling foe of such strategies; see, for example, "Why I Cannot Support the Common Core Standards," *Diane Ravitch's Blog*, 26 February 2013, available online at https://dianeravitch.net/2013/02/26/why-i-cannot-support-the-common-core-standards/.

Notes to Chapter One

1 Rousseau, *Emile*, 172.

2 Quoted in Roger Scruton, "The Idea of a University," *American Spectator*, 17 September 2010, available online at http://spectator.org/articles/38984/idea-university.

3 Martin Heidegger, *What Is Called Thinking?* Religious Perspectives 21 (New York: Harper & Row, 1968), 15. "Teaching is more difficult than learning because what teaching calls for is this: to let learn." A colleague of mine, when I showed him this quote, remarked, "This is rich, coming from Heidegger!" Indeed, for a number of reasons, we might not think of Heidegger as an exemplar of this sentiment.

4 Karl Marx, *Economic and Philosophic Manuscripts of 1844* (New York: International Publishers, 1964), 169.

5 As Marx put it, "I am ugly, but I can buy for myself the most beautiful of women. Therefore I am not ugly, for the effect of ugliness … is nullified by money." Ibid., 167.

6 Ibid., 108.

7 Such a desire does not rule out other motivations to teach – in particular, the desire to see our students do well.

8 Ken Bain, *What the Best College Teachers Do* (Cambridge, MA: Harvard University Press, 2004), 153.

9 Duane F. Shell et al., *The Unified Learning Model: How Motivational, Cognitive, and Neurobiological Sciences Inform Best Teaching Practices* (Dordrecht, Netherlands: Springer, 2010), 7.

10 According to Shell et al., "[w]orking memory allocation is directed by motivation" and is one of the three basic principles of learning (ibid., 3).

11 Susan A. Ambrose et al., *How Learning Works: Seven Research-Based Principles for Smart Teaching* (San Francisco: Jossey-Bass, 2010), 3, emphasis in original.

12 Shell et al., *Unified Learning Model*, 15.

13 James E. Zull, "The Art of Changing the Brain," *Educational Leadership* 62, no. 1 (2004): 69.

14 Ibid., 70. Elsewhere Zull writes, "[e]motion is the foundation of learning. The chemicals of emotion act by modifying the strength and contribution of each part of the learning cycle. Their impact is directly on the signaling systems in each affected neuron"; see idem, "Key Aspects of How the Brain Learns," *New Directions for Adult & Continuing Education* 2006, no. 110 (2006): 7. Shell et al. offer a similar explanation: "The brain areas associated with working memory have substantial connections with the brain areas associated with emotions. This means that working memory is receiving significant input from emotions. These emotional inputs can affect attention and how the capacity that working memory has is allocated"; Shell et al., *Unified Learning Model*, 13.

15 Zull, "Art of Changing the Brain," 70.

16 A few years ago, I was confronted with one such student. In explaining why she liked her math class so much, she said something to the effect of "the class showed me what math was all about. I used to hate math, but this class made me do a complete 360."

17 I make no exceptions here for disciplines in which knowledge builds cumulatively, such that understanding at each level requires understanding at prior levels. It is true that, in such disciplines, students cannot move beyond a step without having grasped the one they are on, but notice that I am discussing what students must do, not what we, their teachers, must do.

18 Many will recognize this language as that of Bloom's famous taxonomy; see Benjamin Samuel Bloom, *Taxonomy of Educational Objectives: The Classification of Educational Goals* (New York: Longmans, Green, 1956).

19 I can report from personal experience that university students in the 1970s (of which I was one) were hardly models of academic virtue.

20 For a lucid and brief discussion of such mechanisms (in the context of "self-efficacy"), see Albert Bandura, "Exercise of Personal and Collective Efficacy in Changing Societies," in *Self-Efficacy in Changing Societies*, ed. Albert Bandura (Cambridge: Cambridge University Press, 1995), 1–13.

21 Behind the critical intentions of those who use this term lies a basic misconception of the word "entertain." The literal meaning – "to carry with" – captures quite well the ideals of education.

22 Virginia Brackett, "Inspiring Student Self-Motivation," *InSight: A Collection of Faculty Scholarship* 2 (2007): 26.

23 For a wonderful chart that displays teaching methods and their corresponding levels of learning, see Linda B. Nilson, *Teaching at Its Best: A Research-Based Resource for College Instructors*, 3rd ed. (San Francisco: Jossey-Bass, 2010), 107.

24 For an account of my own attempt to teach an entire semester without speaking a word in class, see my "Looking Back (and Forward) on Rousseau's *Emile*," *Journal of Political Science Education* 12, no. 4 (2016): 487–97.

25 So Brackett's observation that "[a] student who lacks a sense of identity and desire to learn may fail to self-motivate despite our best efforts to inspire" is little more than a truism and hardly a call to inaction; "Inspiring Student Self-Motivation," 31.

26 See, for example, Brian C. Patrick et al., "'What's Everybody So Excited About?': The Effects of Teacher Enthusiasm on Student Intrinsic Motivation and Vitality," *Journal of Experimental Education* 68, no. 3 (2000): 217.

27 As with most topics in university teaching, the classic texts of the trade provide the most basic and quickest overviews of the motivational literature. See, in particular, Wilbert James McKeachie and Marilla D. Svinicki, *McKeachie's Teaching Tips: Strategies, Research, and Theory for College and University Teachers*, 13th ed. (Belmont, CA: Wadsworth, Cengage Learning, 2011), chap. 11; Barbara Gross Davis, *Tools for Teaching* (San Francisco: Jossey-Bass, 2001), chap. 31;

and Nilson, *Teaching at Its Best*, chap. 5. In what follows, I draw on these books, and on Ambrose, *How Learning Works*, chap. 3; Brackett, "Inspiring Student Self-Motivation"; Frank Pajares, "Toward a Positive Psychology of Academic Motivation," *Journal of Educational Research* 95, no. 1 (October 9, 2001): 27–35; Zull, "Art of Changing the Brain"; idem, "Key Aspects of How the Brain Learns"; and the articles in special issues of *Contemporary Educational Psychology* 25, no. 1 (2000) and *Educational Psychology Review* 13, no. 2 (2001).

28 Even though we don't cause student learning in the traditional sense of learning, all the items are consistent with basic principles of good teaching. For more on this point, see, for example, A.W. Chickering and Z.F. Gamson, "Seven Principles for Good Practice in Undergraduate Education," *AAHE Bulletin* 39, no. 7 (1987): 3–7; and José Antonio Bowen, *Teaching Naked: How Moving Technology Out of Your College Classroom Will Improve Student Learning* (San Francisco: Jossey-Bass, 2012), 85.

29 Cf. Nilson, *Teaching at Its Best*, 51.

30 "Rather than explaining ideas or correcting errors, we may find ourselves more able to trust in learning. This means allowing learners to develop their own representations, theories, and actions instead of attempting to transfer our knowledge to them. Educators cannot give their ideas to adult learners like birthday presents" (Zull, "Key Aspects of How the Brain Learns," 8). For a good overview of intrinsic motivation, see Richard M. Ryan and Edward L. Deci, "Intrinsic and Extrinsic Motivations: Classic Definitions and New Directions," *Contemporary Educational Psychology* 25, no. 1 (2000): 54–67. Zull ("Art of Changing the Brain," 70) offers the following bit of neurological support: "Neuroscience tells us that the positive emotions in learning are generated in the parts of the brain that are used most heavily when students develop their own ideas ... The biochemical rewards of learning are not provided by explanation but by students' ownership."

31 My enthusiasm for intrinsic motivation should in no way be viewed as a condemnation of the extrinsic sort, the judicious use of which can be highly effective. On this point, see Bowen, *Teaching Naked*, 94, and James M. Lang, *Cheating Lessons: Learning from Academic Dishonesty* (Cambridge, MA: Harvard University Press, 2013).

32 Finkel points out that much of what is learned is also in the absence of *teachers*; see *Teaching with Your Mouth Shut*, 6–7.

33 B.F. Skinner was correct – although not in the way he intended – to say that teaching is passing the buck.

34 I explore this idea in more detail in Peter Lindsay, "Abstract Teaching for a Concrete World: A Lesson from Plato," *PS: Political Science & Politics* 44, no. 3 (2011): 605–10.

35 For an excellent overview on promoting civility, especially in larger classes, see Mary Deane Sorcinelli, "Promoting Civility in Large Classes," in *Engaging Large Classes: Strategies and Techniques for College Faculty*, ed. Christine A. Stanley and M. Erin Porter, 44–57 (Boston: Anker, 2002).

36 For an excellent overview of feedback on writing, see John C. Bean and Maryellen Weimer, *Engaging Ideas: The Professor's Guide to Integrating Writing, Critical Thinking, and Active Learning in the Classroom*, 2nd ed. (San Francisco: Jossey-Bass, 2011), chap. 16.

37 See Davis, *Tools for Teaching*; McKeachie and Svinicki, *McKeachie's Teaching Tips*; Nilson, *Teaching at Its Best*.

Notes to Chapter Two

1 Ambrose et al., *How Learning Works*, 218. The authors, I should note, deny the truth of this statement.

2 Bain, *What the Best College Teachers Do.*

3 Ironically, one could interpret the original cover of Bain's book – a picture of a university professor doing a one-hand handstand – as making precisely this point.

4 Kenneth Eugene Eble, *The Craft of Teaching: A Guide to Mastering the Professor's Art* (San Francisco: Jossey-Bass, 1976), 13.

5 The psychological dynamic between the person and the persona one takes on is not something I wish – or am able – to explain. That said, it is tempting to speculate wildly. Perhaps some classroom behaviors reflect sublimated guilt over *not* having these traits in the course of, say, one's family life. Or perhaps having virtues such as patience or respectfulness in the classroom *results* in not having them elsewhere, as if the supply is depleted as soon as the classroom bell rings. Educational research needs a book equivalent to Harold Lasswell's, *Psychopathology and Politics* (Chicago: University of Chicago Press, [1930] 1977), a fascinating if speculative attempt to explain political personalities through a psychoanalytic framework.

6 See Aristotle, *Nicomachean Ethics*, 2nd ed. (Indianapolis: Hackett, 1999), bk. II.

7 Another somewhat more mundane example of adopting a persona has to do with clothing. When I started teaching, I was twenty-six and in need of something to assure myself that I was the teacher, not another student. I decided to wear a tie. Somewhat surprisingly, it helped more than almost anything else I did. I should note that this example is hardly gender neutral, for, as a reader of this manuscript put it, it "raises the distinction between male and female professors and how they are scrutinized differently by students and colleagues on the basis of their appearance." I agree. Rather than (as the reader suggested) dropping the example, I think it better to leave it as a marker of sorts, one that indicates an excellent starting point for a discussion that I have ignored completely, but that emphatically needs to be addressed: the issues this matter of personas raises for gender (and race). I welcome readers' thoughts on the matter.

8 In truth I could have suggested that he start *being* that person, for in a sense that's what I meant. I did not, however, since at that moment I was a faculty developer, not a pedagogical critic – a different persona.

9 Paulo Freire, *Pedagogy of the Oppressed*, 20th anniversary ed. (New York: Continuum, 1993).

10 Parker J. Palmer, *The Courage to Teach: Exploring the Inner Landscape of a Teacher's Life* (San Francisco: Jossey-Bass, 1998), 10. Reinsmith also has very similar ideas; see William A. Reinsmith, *Archetypal Forms in Teaching: A Continuum*, Contributions to the Study of Education 56 (New York: Greenwood Press, 1992). See also bell hooks, *Teaching to Transgress: Education as the Practice of Freedom* (New York: Routledge, 1994), 15, 18.

11 Elbe suggests that distaste among education researchers for the related topic of teaching style might stem from the fact that "it has been confused with affectation, denigrated as a kind of posturing to mask a lack of substance, or tolerated as a natural manifestation of personal eccentricities"; quoted in Anthony Grasha, *Teaching with Style: A Practical Guide to Enhancing Learning by Understanding Teaching and Learning Styles* (San Bernardino, CA: Alliance, 2002), 1.

12 The academic literature that does address teaching personalities (or "styles" or "types") offers a number of ways to think about the matter. As Grasha (ibid., 38–9) points out, research distinguishes between general modes of classroom behavior (teachers' ability to do certain things, such as generate excitement); the personal characteristics of successful teachers; the methods they employ (lecturer, discussion leader, case study facilitator); the roles they play (expert, evaluator, materials designer); the mode of student-teacher interaction; and personality traits (extrovert or introvert). Even metaphors through which teachers see themselves (as matadors, evangelists, midwives, entertainers, gardeners) are used. Although this literature focuses on individuals *qua* teachers – or, as in the case of the Jungian-inspired Myers-Briggs Type Indicator personality inventory, is *applied* to teachers from larger personality studies; see Isabel Briggs Myers, *Introduction to Type: A Guide to Understanding Your Results on the Myers-Briggs Type Indicator*, 6th ed. (Palo Alto, CA: Consulting Psychologists Press, 1998) – it generally avoids treating any such behaviors as matters separate from the individual. Personalities are not seen as tools to be used so much as dispositions that we observe. Formulations of style are mostly descriptive, and as such are devoid of suggestions regarding "the specific actions someone might take to adopt, enhance, or modify the style they already possess" (Grasha, *Teaching with Style*, 39). Even Reinsmith, in his description of the "continuum" through which teachers move, suggests that movement will come more as a result of one's natural progression over years of teaching than as a deliberate and conscious attempt to move from one "archetypal form" to the next: "Most often, change … is catalyzed by a dissatisfaction with the current level of encounter and subsequent learning that is taking place. The teacher

feels cramped, frustrated, distanced from her students. A more personal, intimate connection is sought ... To an extent the attitudes and skills required for each new mode will flow naturally out of the new vision of teaching possibility arising in the teacher. They are intrinsic to the new form in the sense that the teacher will understand intuitively what skills must be learned"; see Reinsmith, *Archetypal Forms in Teaching*, 173–5. Moreover, whatever change occurs in this process does not directly involve a classroom persona. For a related discussion about "identity," see Carol R. Rodgers and Katherine H. Scott, "The Personal Self and Professional Identity in Learning to Teach," in *Handbook of Research on Teacher Education: Enduring Questions in Changing Contexts*, ed. Marilyn Cochran-Smith et al. (New York: Routledge, 2008), 732–55.

13 Grasha, *Teaching with Style*, 40.

14 Quoted in ibid.

15 Ibid., 1.

16 I am indebted to a reviewer for prompting me to make this distinction clear.

17 I should acknowledge here the concern voiced by a reviewer – namely, that putting on a persona might, for an experienced teacher, be "exhausting and a recipe for burnout." Indeed, it *can* be exhausting, and perhaps for some it does indeed lead to burnout. My hope, however, is that it might, in offering a new perspective on the classroom, have the opposite effect.

18 Empathy was a trait I inferred from the fact that, when energy levels flagged or confusion reigned, the instructor seemed to pick up on it.

19 Although one teacher, who admitted she was nervous, conducted the class from the exact same spot in the room without so much as lifting a foot during the entire seventy-five minutes.

20 It might be more accurate to say they had a sense of humor. Often, this sense came out not in the cracking of jokes, but in the ability to see and play upon the humor that was created (via student comments, awkward situations, technology breakdowns) in the room.

21 Joseph Lowman offers an interesting parallel to my observations in his analysis of the common adjectives used to describe nominees for teaching awards; see "Professors as Performers and Motivators," *College Teaching* 42, no. 4 (1994): 137–41.

22 Enthusiasm can be expressed in subtle ways. One colleague began class by saying, "today we'll only have time to do two things." I don't know why that caught my attention; perhaps I heard in his voice a sense of regret that there was not more time. Somehow it sounded like "I have two great surprises for you." It certainly sounded very different than the perfunctory "now let's look at a couple of poems."

23 Socrates' claim (in Plato's *Apology*) that the realization of ignorance is a sign of wisdom has its limits, for if one is paralyzed by that realization, all learning might cease. In his case, at least, Socrates warded off despondency by further understanding that what he *did* know was at least as much as what others knew.

24 I discuss this idea in the context of requiring attendance in Peter Lindsay, "Attending to Attendance," *Chronicle of Higher Education*, 4 February 2015, available online at http://www.chronicle.com/blogs/conversation/2015/02/04/attending-to-attendance/, accessed 14 December 14.

25 L. Dee Fink, *Creating Significant Learning Experiences: An Integrated Approach to Designing College Courses*, 2nd ed. (San Francisco: Jossey-Bass, 2013).

26 As Reinsmith (*Archetypal Forms in Teaching*, xi–xii) puts it: "At best, teaching is a process of creating different encounters by which students can learn and thus come to know … Successful teaching (which issues in learning) connotes a partnership, even a communality, of a special kind … A teaching encounter is not simply a group of skills or methods assembled in a particular way. It may engender these, but the 'meeting' between teacher and student(s) has a form or being of its own."

27 Ask whether you are curious to know the details and, if so, what this means for your judgment of me – or, for that matter, what it means about *you*. Then ask if you should teach.

28 In Chapter Five I discuss the moral failings that *do* have bearing on student learning.

Notes to Chapter Three

1 The results of at least one study confirm this disheartening assumption: "46% of students reported that they read assignments, yet only 55% of those students were able to demonstrate the most basic level of comprehension of the material they claimed to have read." Mary Hoeft, "Why University Students Don't Read: What Professors Can Do to Increase Compliance," *International Journal for the Scholarship of Teaching and Learning* 6, no. 2 (2012), available online at http://digitalcommons.georgiasouthern.edu/ij-sotl/vol6/iss2/12/, accessed 8 December 2016.

2 The complete letter can be found at University of California, Irvine, UCI Libraries, available online at http://ucispace.lib.uci.edu/bitstream/handle/10575/1094/16DeManPortableRousseauMalesherbes.pdf?sequence=22.

3 Karl Sabbagh, *The Riemann Hypothesis: The Greatest Unsolved Problem in Mathematics*, reprint ed. (New York: Farrar, Straus and Giroux, 2004), 50.

4 Jim Holt, "He Conceived the Mathematics of Roughness," *New York Review of Books*, 23 May 2013.

5 John R. Searle, "The Mystery of Consciousness Continues," *New York Review of Books*, 9 June 2011, available online at http://www.nybooks.com/articles/2011/06/09/mystery-consciousness-continues/, accessed 15 December 2016. Searle gives another explanation of these distinctions in "Can Information Theory Explain Consciousness?" *New York Review of Books*, 10 January 2013, available online at http://www.nybooks.com/articles/2013/01/10/can-information-theory-explain-consciousness/, accessed 15 December 2016.

6 The ability to relate to a subject is at the far end of a spectrum that is crucial for reading ability: the knowledge the reader has in the subject about which she is reading. As Daniel Willingham reports, "students who score well on reading tests are those with broad knowledge; they usually know at least a little about the topics of the passages on the test"; see Daniel T. Willingham, "How to get your mind to read," *New York Times*, 25 November 2017, available online at https://www.nytimes.com/2017/11/25/opinion/ sunday/how-to-get-your-mind-to-read.html?action=click&pgtype=Homepage&clickSo urce=story-heading&module=region&region=region&WT.nav=region&_r=2, accessed 2 December 2017. I would suggest that the ability to relate to a subject is closely tied to the knowledge base we have for it. For an excellent account of this and other cognitive issues surrounding reading, see Daniel T. Willingham, *The Reading Mind: A Cognitive Approach to Understanding How the Mind Reads* (San Francisco: Jossey-Bass, 2017).

7 I have not discussed a few important related topics – in particular, preparing students for the readings and ways to sell them on those readings, and giving them tools to increase their comprehension. Linda Nilson does a wonderful job on both; see *Teaching at Its Best*, chap. 23.

Notes to Chapter Four

1 Jacques Ellul, *The Technological Society*, trans. John Wilkinson (New York: Vintage Books, 1964), 6.

2 As a report by the US Department of Education makes clear, the current trend is in precisely the opposite direction; see Alexandria Walton Radford, "Learning at a Distance: Undergraduate Enrollment in Distance Education Courses and Degree Programs," Statistics in Brief NCES 2012-154 (Washington, DC: Department of Education, October 2011), available online at http://nces.ed.gov/pubs2012/2012154. pdf. For the department's evaluation of this trend's effect on learning, see Barbara Means et al., "Evaluation of Evidence-Based Practices in Online Learning: A Meta-Analysis and Review of Online Learning Studies" (Washington, DC: Department of Education Office of Planning, Evaluation, and Policy Development, Policy and Program Studies Service, September 2010), available online at http://www2.ed.gov/ rschstat/eval/tech/evidence-based-practices/finalreport.pdf.

3 For a good discussion of the debate over such research, see Matt Richtel, "Technology in schools faces questions on value," *New York Times*, 3 September 2011, available online at http://www.nytimes.com/2011/09/04/technology/ technology-in-schools-faces-questions-on-value.html.

4 It should not surprise us that the trend of the past thirty years in American primary and secondary education toward increased testing has been visibly supported by the technology industries that administer these tests. Given the failure of this testing philosophy to improve American education, even by its own standards, we might reasonably ask if the desired result was better education or higher profit.

5 This trend explains why administrators willingly throw at technology the amounts of money they do without a *shred* of evidence about learning outcomes. Technology is unique in this regard. Ask yourself how many programs on your campus get funded before the research on their effects is done. Better yet, how many programs get funded *with the purpose* of finding out if they're effective?

6 In my work as a faculty developer, I would frequently, after discussing with an instructor the alternative methods of engaging students with the course material, hear, "but I can't really PowerPoint that."

7 Perhaps you've heard an advocate for one of these systems report (usually with glee) that, "if you just hit this button you can get a report of how many times your students have logged on!!"

8 One of the more dramatic examples of technology's hold on education is Bowen's remarkable claim – made in the midst of an otherwise reasonable discussion of how to use technology in education – that, "[i]f you do not have both LinkedIn and Facebook profiles, if you do not tweet or blog (or know that a tweet is like a Facebook status update), if you do not routinely use iTunes or YouTube, if you do not know how to use GPS, or if you do not share photos on Flickr, Snapfish, or Picasa, then you have an immediate credibility problem with your students" (Bowen, *Teaching Naked*, 30). To my thinking, credibility comes in all forms, and there are insurmountable hurdles to some of them. I will, for instance, never again be twenty-something and I will never ever be female or African American or gay. Perhaps these facts about me will create credibility problems with respect to certain subjects and certain students. But does that mean I have a credibility problem *per se*? Writ large? And where exactly does this credibility problem rate next to one I might bring on if the gaps in my knowledge were actually about the subject matter of the course? Indeed, it's odd that credibility here is linked to facts about a teacher's personal life that are quite irrelevant from a pedagogical or even an academic perspective.

9 For a good analysis of PowerPoint's educational shortcomings, see Edward R. Tufte, *The Cognitive Style of PowerPoint: Pitching Out Corrupts Within*, 2nd ed. (Cheshire, CT: Graphics Press, 2006). In the interest of being "fair and balanced," I draw readers' attention to a defense of PowerPoint by Tad Simons, "Does PowerPoint Make You Stupid?" *Presentations.com*, March 2004, available online at http://www.ltrr.arizona.edu/kkh/dendro/PDFs.Tufte/Does%20PowerPoint%20Make%20you%20Stupid.pdf. Simons rightly points out that the problem is not with the medium but with its use. What I think he overlooks is the point I have just made: the medium facilitates and even encourages that use. The article quotes Cliff Atkinson: "Tufte is right to criticize PowerPoint paradigms that result in people presenting certain types of information in limiting, linear ways. But there is no reason why PowerPoint has to be used in ways Tufte describes." Simons continues: "The notion that PowerPoint exercises some sort of punitive, authoritarian power over presenters – a power that can't be resisted – is pure bunk, Atkinson says." If there is bunk here, it is with the

idea that no reasons exist to explain why PowerPoint is presented in limiting, linear ways. One need not grant PowerPoint "punitive, authoritarian power." (Indeed, I know of no one who does.) All one needs to accept is that PowerPoint, like all technology, has a tendency to encourage certain ways of accomplishing the tasks to which we put it. Defenders cannot have it both ways: conceding that PowerPoint does – commonly – result in the poor practices that Tufte describes precludes one from laying the blame on hapless users. Still, until PowerPoint goes away, the best response is, as with all drugs, to promote responsible use. A good place to start is with a list of suggestions collected by Chris Clark, "Seven (+?) Resources for Better PowerPoint," *NspireD2: Learning Technology in Higher Ed.*, 1 February 2011, available online at https://ltlatnd.wordpress.com/2011/02/01/seven-resources-for-better-powerpoint/, and posted on the Kaneb Center website: http://ltlatnd.wordpress.com/2011/02/01/seven-resources-for-better-powerpoint/.

10 Such bombarding can easily result in what's known as "cognitive overload." For an excellent treatment of the issue, with some helpful suggestions, see Richard E. Mayer and Roxana Moreno, "Nine Ways to Reduce Cognitive Load in Multimedia Learning," *Educational Psychologist* 38, no. 1 (2003): 43–52.

11 For example, students who have trouble articulating their thoughts in a classroom setting surely would benefit from being asked to develop those thoughts at least well enough to post a cogent paragraph or two on a discussion board.

12 I fully accept the possibility that these words will seem quaint in fifty or so years. For now, however – and for the immediate future – we still confront much of life, of reality, face to face. That fact should not go unnoticed when we reflect upon the social interaction with which people learn. At a minimum, it seems tame enough to insist that education should be conducted in the language of life.

13 This claim is not contradicted by Bowen's observations that "human beings are experimenting with new definitions of social proximity" and that "[o]nline social networking means that relationships and communication no longer depend on physical contact." Indeed, the thrust of Bowen's argument is that we must use technology to preserve "student face time with faculty in the classroom" – what he calls "our most precious asset of nontechnological faculty" (Bowen, *Teaching Naked*, 187).

14 In a vivid example of how misguided that thought is, Nancy Bunge comments that, in her course evaluations, students who were in the course with no online component "talked about my enthusiasm, respect for their opinions, and obsession with making sure that understood the texts and assignments – all traits beyond a computer's reach … Studying my students' reactions reminds me that teaching well means participating in a relationship with them. Apparently, turning over a fourth of the course to a computer weakened the bond between us, even though every week I wrote individual responses to their online work." See Nancy Bunge, "Why I No Longer Teach Online," *Chronicle of Higher Education*," 6 November 2011,

available online at http://www.chronicle.com/article/Why-I-No-Longer-Teach-Online/129615/, accessed 15 December 2016.

15 Brenau University, a for-profit institute in Atlanta, captured the thought well with an advertisement featuring the following student testimonial: "In my opinion, the greatest thing about online education is that I do not have to sacrifice so much family time in an actual classroom. I am able to multitask family and school." This student might as well have said he was glad that he didn't have to sacrifice so much family time to learning. Or better yet: "It was great – I didn't have to open my mind at all. Critical reflection?! With three kids and a mortgage?"

16 As Stanley Fish has put it, "[a] new technology typically turns its limitations into a mechanism of evaluation and consigns phenomena outside its capacities to the margins, not merely to its margins but to the margins of what is generally significant and worth worrying about"; see Stanley Eugene Fish, "The two cultures of educational reform," *New York Times*, 26 August 2013, available online at http://opinionator.blogs.nytimes.com/2013/08/26/the-two-cultures-of-educational-reform/?_r=0, accessed 15 December 2016.

17 Think, for instance, of how frequently we hear classrooms disparaged for their "one-size-fits-all" limitations. And think how limit*ed* that view really is: although it's true that, in a classroom, students cannot easily go at their own pace – a virtue rightly celebrated by educational websites such as that of the Kahn Academy – sometimes in education that fact is precisely the point. What those websites cannot easily tap into is the crucial element of student-centered education, the element that treats as a virtue the requirement of moving together *as a group*. (For a supportive yet critical look at Kahn Academy's educational potential, see Robert Talbert, "The Trouble with Khan Academy – Casting Out Nines," *Chronicle of Higher Education*, 3 July 2012, available online at http://www.chronicle.com/blognetwork/castingoutnines/2012/07/03/the-trouble-with-khan-academy/, accessed 15 December 2016.)

18 Perhaps the farthest reaching technological distortion of education is with respect to education's perceived goals. Think, for example, of arguments for various technologies that point out how much students *like* glitzy things or that these glitzy things *engage* students. The problem with such pitches that, although students might indeed like glitz, that fact on its own does not count as a reason to employ it – we would first need to demonstrate that this preference translates into learning (that like = learning). They might like it if they could bring small televisions to class with them – so what? Even the fact that students are engaged by a technological tool doesn't mean much unless the engagement is of the right sort. To put the matter simply: it is not the mission of educators to give students what they like or what will engage them, and it is a mark of how poor the technologists' arguments are that words such as "like" and "engage" have become proxies for "learn," without in many cases even the slightest attempt to demonstrate that a correlation exists.

19 See, for example, G. Christensen et al., "The MOOC Phenomenon: Who Takes Massive Open Online Courses and Why?" SSRN Scholarly Paper (Rochester, NY: Social Science Research Network, November 2013), available online at http://papers.ssrn.com/abstract=2350964.

20 Ellul, *Technological Society*, xxix.

21 Fermat's famous theorem – that there are no integers above 2 for which x raised to that integer plus y raised to it equals z raised to it – offers a clear illustration of the distinction. It is easy to see that the equation will not work for any number we try, but one would not presume from all the trying that we could ever say there were *no* numbers among the infinite possibilities for which it was true. To make the latter assertion, one would have to show why no number *could be* found – that is, why it is *mathematically* impossible.

22 As I explain below, Euclid's proof was geometric, and in what follows I translate it into the more recent mathematical language of algebra.

23 This remark is of pedagogical importance: it is always a good thing to share one's excitement about a topic with students, even – or especially – if it makes you look at bit nerdy.

24 G.H. Hardy, *A Mathematician's Apology* (1940; repr. Cambridge: Cambridge University, 1969), 94.

25 A quick caveat: no single experience is optimal for all students. The key is to find the experience that works best for a group with diverse abilities.

26 I should note that this analysis is meant to supplement, not contradict, the analysis of the chapter on teaching personas.

27 Of course, for some students, comprehension might come best by simply reading the proof on their own. This does not mean that, for them, the class is a waste of time, only that *this element* of the class would not bring to these students the same benefits it would to others.

28 The key is actually not the visualization, but the memory of it – how we construct it in our mind; see Tracey Tokuhama-Espinosa, *Mind, Brain, and Education Science: A Comprehensive Guide to the New Brain-Based Teaching* (New York: W.W. Norton, 2011), 40. As such there might be instances when actual visualizing is unnecessary. Indeed, we should not overplay the importance of visualization. PowerPoint's allure comes in part from the mistaken impression that students cannot learn in the absence of visual cues. There might, in fact, be times when we would do well *not* to provide visual representations of things. In certain instances, denying this input might force students to grapple more vigorously with understanding. It also might lead to internally created representations – the process of "imagining" rather than "imaging" a process that, in the end, activates the same parts of the visual cortex – see David A. Sousa, *How the Brain Learns: A Classroom Teacher's Guide* (Thousand Oaks, CA: Corwin Press, 2001), 235 – rather than those imposed externally. Think, for instance, of the representations we create when we read a

novel, and what happens to them when we see the film adaptation. Would we understand better what Anthony Burgess was saying in *A Clockwork Orange* by constructing an image of Alex (the protagonist) from our reading the book or by accepting Malcolm McDowell's portrayal in Stanley Kubrick's film version? For more on visualization, see A.F. Helene and G.F. Xavier, "Working Memory and Acquisition of Implicit Knowledge by Imagery Training, without Actual Task Performance," *Neuroscience* 139, no. 1 (2006): 401–13; A. Mazard et al., "Neural Impact of the Semantic Content of Visual Mental Images and Visual Percepts," *Cognitive Brain Research* 24, no. 3 (2005): 423–35; and William L. Thompson et al., "Two Forms of Spatial Imagery: Neuroimaging Evidence," *Psychological Science* 20, no. 10 (2009): 1245–53. For an interesting discussion of how visualization affects moral judgments, see Elinor Amit and Joshua D. Greene, "You See, the Ends Don't Justify the Means: Visual Imagery and Moral Judgment," *Psychological Science* 23, no. 8 (2012): 861–8.

29 Actually, it's the chalk I love, perhaps because the dust it leaves behind is the leading destroyer of all the other technology in a classroom. You have to respect a technology that actively seeks to destroy anything that threatens to replace it. As a philosopher, my only question is whether this is a conscious effort.

30 To appreciate fully the experience of your students, consider how infrequently conference presenters leave slides up for the amount of time necessary to transcribe them in some manner.

31 To point out only the most glaring methodological flaw, the whiteboard was clearly advantaged in coming after the PowerPoint presentation.

32 This lack of presence explains why it is hazardous to read a lecture from a script as opposed to constructing aural prose from notes. As I learned reading bedtime stories to my children, it is quite possible to read words on a page without giving their meaning a moment's thought. Constructing coherent thoughts from notes, on the other hand, requires focus, and it is just that focus that keeps the instructor in the same time zone as her students.

33 Of course, a rectangle on paper is a representation of a rectangle in space, so in one respect it itself is removed from a thing. Still, a rectangle on paper *is* something in the way that x is not.

34 It would look like the number line above, except that we would replace 3 with x and 5 with $(x + 2)$. $x^2 + 2x$ would occur where 15 is on the line.

35 Although, to be sure, the differences in learning experiences could in turn be rooted in different cognitive abilities.

36 On the importance of such diversity, see Bain, *What the Best College Teachers Do*, 116–17; McKeachie and Svinicki, *McKeachie's Teaching Tips*, 168; Judy Willis, *Research-based Strategies to Ignite Student Learning: Insights from a Neurologist and Classroom Teacher* (Alexandria, VA: Association for Supervision and Curriculum Development, 2006), 90; Daniel T. Willingham, *Why Don't Students Like School?*

A Cognitive Scientist Answers Questions about How the Mind Works and What It Means for the Classroom (San Francisco: Jossey-Bass, 2009), 114–27; and Donald A. Bligh, *What's the Use of Lectures?* (Exeter, UK: Intellect, 1998), 257. I should note that the idea that there exist different learning styles is far from settled. In fact, one thorough study on the matter concludes: "The contrast between the enormous popularity of the learning-styles approach within education and the lack of credible evidence for its utility is, in our opinion, striking and disturbing. If classification of students' learning styles has practical utility, it remains to be demonstrated"; see Harold Pashler et al., "Learning Styles: Concepts and Evidence," *Psychological Science in the Public Interest* 9, no. 3 (2008): 117. In its typical fashion, the *Onion* captured the hype surrounding learning styles well with its headline: "Parents Of Nasal Learners Demand Odor-Based Curriculum" (*Onion*, 15 March 2000, available online at https://www.theonion.com/parents-of-nasal-learners-demand-odor-based-curriculum-1819565536).

37 For a discussion of the detrimental effects of the laptop, see Helene Hembrooke and Geri Gay, "The Laptop and the Lecture: The Effects of Multitasking in Learning Environments," *Journal of Computing in Higher Education* 15, no. 1 (2003): 46–64. Sana et al. point to the fact that laptops are detrimental not just to the user, but also to those nearby; see Faria Sana, Tina Weston, and Nicholas J. Cepeda, "Laptop Multitasking Hinders Classroom Learning for Both Users and Nearby Peers," *Computers & Education* 62 (2013): 24–31. For evidence that long-forgotten longhand might be preferable to laptop keyboards, see Pam A. Mueller and Daniel M. Oppenheimer, "The Pen Is Mightier Than the Keyboard Advantages of Longhand Over Laptop Note Taking," *Psychological Science*, 23 April 2014, available online at https://sites.udel.edu/victorp/files/2010/11/Psychological-Science-2014-Mueller-0956797614524581-1u0h0yu.pdf.

Notes to Chapter Five

1 I did, however, neglect to mention it at the interview for my first teaching job – as history teacher at a high school outside Boston. As my university transcript lacked even one history course, I'm sure the question came up as to my credentials as a historian and, given that the course I am describing here was that last one I had taken, I shudder to think about the creative answer I might have given. Whatever it was must have worked, as I got the job and began (finally) learning history, doing so in the most effective manner I know: by teaching it.

2 Davis, *Tools for Teaching*, 302–4.

3 J.M. Roberts, *History of the World* (New York: Oxford University Press, 1993), 845. Note that the citations to Roberts in the exercise are to an earlier edition.

4 In a fascinating study of paraphrasing practices among academics, Miguel Roig concludes that "there can be substantial differences in how paraphrasing and

plagiarism are defined even with in a single discipline. At a time when university faculty and administrations are drawing increasing attention to the problem of plagiarism in the academy, the current situation represents a highly undesirable state of affairs in need of immediate attention." See Miguel Roig, "Plagiarism and Paraphrasing Criteria of College and University Professors," *Ethics & Behavior* 11, no. 3 (2001): 321.

5 For a good example of the gray area, see Christopher Shea, "When One Biographer 'Borrows' from Another, the Dispute Gets Philosophical," *Chronicle of Higher Education*, 9 July 2012, available online at http://www.chronicle.com/article/When-One-Biographer-Borrows/132705/A. This topic is explored in some depth in Susan Debra Blum, *My Word! Plagiarism and College Culture* (Ithaca, NY: Cornell University Press, 2010).

6 Oliver Sacks draws an insightful distinction between plagiarism and "cryptomnesia," the borrowing of ideas or words (or melodies) that is neither conscious nor intentional but that results from our quite common and unwitting appropriation of other people's creations as our own. We read a text or hear a song and, much later, have it resurface as something original to us. Childhood memories are a prime example, and Sacks reports discovering how he had come to "remember" an incident from his childhood that in fact had been reported to him in a vivid letter from his brother. See Oliver Sacks, "Speak, Memory," *New York Review of Books*, 21 February 2013, available online at https://www.nybooks.com/articles/2013/02/21/speak-memory/, accessed 13 December 2016.

7 On the causes and cures of cheating, the classic textbooks on university teaching are probably the best resources for most educators, as they draw from and distill the academic research in readable and usable form. Three good choices are McKeachie and Svinicki, *McKeachie's Teaching Tips*; Davis, *Tools for Teaching*; and Nilson, *Teaching at Its Best*. For those who want a more thorough and complete (and excellent) overview, see Lang, *Cheating Lessons*.

8 An astute workshop participant once pointed out that, by inverting the "ch" and the "t" in cheating, we could change a question I put on the board from "What can we do about cheating?" to "What can we do about teaching?" I have since used the trick in numerous workshops, and it never fails to elicit subtle acknowledgement of cleverness for which, in a not so subtle act of performative contraction, I take full credit.

9 Sixty percent of instructors report that cheating happens, but only 20 percent take action. The reasons for the lack of action are no time, no administrative support, and no hard evidence.

10 Lang (*Cheating Lessons*, 39) offers an excellent and extended version of this thesis, put succinctly as follows: "The environments which reduce the incentive and opportunity to cheat are the very ones that, according to the most current information we have about how human beings learn, will lead to greater and deeper learning by your students."

11 Eble, *Craft of Teaching*, 125. Elsewhere he puts the matter more positively: "As a general principle, faith and trust are ultimately beneficial to teaching regardless of how both may be, in specific instances, ill rewarded" (123). Eble points out that, aside from pedagogical considerations, trust also has its practical virtues: "Real proof of cheating on tests constitutes such a thing as clamping a hand on a wrist with the shirt cuffs exposed and the test answers clearly visible thereon. Even then, the alleged criminal may claim it's his roommates shirt. Better to give him a try at another test than strip him of his shirt" (124).

12 Michel de Montaigne, *The Essays: A Selection* (New York: Penguin, 1993), 43–I:26.

13 For an interesting discussion of how academic culture creates an environment conducive to dishonest practices, see David Mcneill, "Japanese Fraud Case Highlights Weaknesses in Scientific Publishing," *Chronicle of Higher Education*, 8 October 2012, available online at http://www.chronicle.com/article/The-Great-Pretender/134876/?cid=at&utm_source=at&utm_medium=en.

14 Aristotle, *Nicomachean Ethics*, bk. III.

15 Here is a reply I have often counselled faculty to give a rewrite-requesting student (in cases where there was no mention of rewrites in the syllabus): "I could perhaps allow you to do that, but first I'd have to contact all of the other students and make the same offer to them." It works like a charm, as students see that it is unreasonable to expect their instructor to make this offer to their peers, while also perceiving that if she does *not* do so, it would be unfair to those peers. I say "perceiving" because, as I've just argued, I'm not sure it really would be unfair. No matter – fairness is more the alibi than the issue here.

16 Lang, *Cheating Lessons*, 7, 13; emphasis in original.

17 For simplicity's sake, I put aside the fact that, in some instances, instructors do not actually have complete control over many aspects of the course they teach. Such is often the case with graduate student teaching, courses with multiple sections, and foundational courses whose learning outcomes are set by licensing boards.

18 For more on these student perspectives and their relationship to cheating, see Tamera B. Murdock and Eric M. Anderman, "Motivational Perspectives on Student Cheating: Toward an Integrated Model of Academic Dishonesty," *Educational Psychologist* 41, no. 3 (2006): 129–45.

19 See Jessica Lahey, "'I Cheated All Throughout High School,'" *Atlantic*, 24 December 2013, available online at http://www.theatlantic.com/education/archive/2013/12/i-cheated-all-throughout-high-school/282566/.

20 I should confess that I've never been much for pillorying cheaters. After all, I can't really take a hard line on the matter – I cheated, remember? For whatever reason, though, I find it hard to take an individual's occasional moral failing as a sign of an irredeemably flawed character. My sympathies here are with Blum,

who, in describing the effects her research on plagiarism had on her view of students, recounts that, "I saw the academic miscreant as more of a lost soul than a hardened criminal" (Blum, *My Word!*, 174). Certainly we can distinguish between a bad person and someone who does a bad thing. It is not, after all, necessarily a sign of *good* character that one *never* commits moral errors or, more remarkably, is never even desirous of doing so. To the contrary, some such person is a freak of nature about whom moral judgment seems inappropriate and who, in any case, is not likely to bless any of our classrooms with her presence.

There is, fortunately, much research that backs up what might seem to be a lax attitude. Studies demonstrate persuasively not only that cheating is tied to the climate in which one finds oneself, but, more important, that nearly *everyone* cheats in one climate or another – particularly where there are few or no negative consequences. See Dan Ariely, *The (Honest) Truth about Dishonesty: How We Lie to Everyone – Especially Ourselves* (New York: Harper, 2012); Blum, *My Word!*; and Jared Piazza, Jesse M. Bering, and Gordon Ingram, "'Princess Alice Is Watching You': Children's Belief in an Invisible Person Inhibits Cheating," *Journal of Experimental Child Psychology* 109, no. 3 (2011): 311–20.

21 Lang, *Cheating Lessons*, 209–10.

22 Ibid., 210.

23 In this regard, zero-tolerance policies are an easy target precisely because they involve an unwillingness to look beyond a narrow range of considerations. Still, I would not rule them out tout court for the same reason I would rule nothing out in this manner: there might be contexts in which the policy is the best option available.

24 Professional schools rightly include ethical behavior as a part of their curriculum, and they do so because knowledge of right and wrong is an integral aspect of being, say, a doctor, lawyer, or accountant.

25 For Lang's compelling rebuttal, see *Cheating Lessons*, 170.

26 Oberlin College is an example; the University of Virginia has a very famous honor code, but it is not student run.

27 We see this level in Eble's (*Craft of Teaching*, 125) claim that, "[t]he fault [for cheating] lies with the overpowering importance attached to locating and transferring facts and opinions and the lack of significance given to thinking and independent expression. The answer is not to move the machinery of formal scholarship down into elementary grades, but to diminish greatly the witless gathering and disguising of facts."

28 We assume, in asking this question, that students are unaware of their professors' blind eyes, for if they knew that cheating had become acceptable, then, absurdly, *whatever* they did would no longer be cheating. (If it is permissible to break a rule, then doing so is not, strictly speaking, breaking it.)

Notes to Chapter Six

1 I should add parenthetically that I have a history of multitasking while driving. I
   don't, as I mentioned earlier, own a cell phone – those are dangerous in cars – but I
   do read maps as I drive. This irritates my wife. She discovered this habit of mine on
   our first trip together, driving through Scotland. She got particularly annoyed when
   she realized at one point that the map on my lap was not *of* Scotland. I had become
   intrigued with the map of the London Underground – in particular, with the fact
   that it takes only one change to get from Turnham Green to Charing Cross. (Who
   knew?)
2 This vision of a simplified life is at the core of manufacturing, a way of producing
   that lies at the opposite extreme from craftwork. Manufacturing is prized precisely
   for its simplified nature, for the fact that individuals can produce with the
   knowledge of only one aspect of the entire process. Frederick Taylor's scientific
   management, with its reduction of tasks to simple, routinized steps requiring no
   creative input of the producer, is perhaps the most vivid illustration of the ideal. Lest
   the enormity of craft production overwhelm us and we cry out for one step and one
   step only, we would do well to recall Adam Smith's observation that work in the pin
   factory, where each job would be limited to one aspect of pin production, would
   make workers as "stupid and ignorant as it is possible for a human creature to be."
   See Adam Smith, *The Theory of Moral Sentiments*, Glasgow Edition of the Works
   and Correspondence of Adam Smith, v. 1 (Oxford: Clarendon Press, 1979), 461. The
   exhaustion that comes with having too much to think about seems far less daunting
   when compared with the stultification brought on by thoughts of nothing at all.
3 That the inspiration for this slogan was Gary Gilmore's request, "Let's do it," made to
   a firing squad with rifles trained at his heart is, I think, telling.
4 If that statement sounds rampantly narcissistic ("crafts as cheap therapy"), bear in
   mind that the craft of teaching is necessarily other-regarding. When we look upon
   ourselves, we gain a healthy sense of our somewhat limited place within the larger
   whole. We juggle various parts of the whole in an effort to maintain a place, but it is
   never at center stage. Students, colleagues, parents – they are all active participants
   in this whole, and their actions cumulatively have a far greater effect on it than do
   ours. Far from diminishing our craft, that fact underscores how many we touch in
   our efforts to practice it.

Works Cited

Ambrose, Susan A., Michael W. Bridges, Marsha C. Lovett, Michele DiPietro, and Marie K. Norman. *How Learning Works: Seven Research-Based Principles for Smart Teaching*. San Francisco: Jossey-Bass, 2010.

Amit, Elinor, and Joshua D. Greene. "You See, the Ends Don't Justify the Means: Visual Imagery and Moral Judgment." *Psychological Science* 23, no. 8 (2012): 861–8. doi:10.1177/0956797611434965.

Ariely, Dan. *The (Honest) Truth about Dishonesty: How We Lie to Everyone – Especially Ourselves*. New York: Harper, 2012.

Aristotle. *Nicomachean Ethics*. 2nd ed. Indianapolis: Hackett, 1999.

Bain, Ken. *What the Best College Teachers Do*. Cambridge, MA: Harvard University Press, 2004.

Bandura, Albert. "Exercise of Personal and Collective Efficacy in Changing Societies." In *Self-Efficacy in Changing Societies*, edited by Albert Bandura, 1–13. Cambridge: Cambridge University Press, 1995.

Barr, Robert B., and John Tagg. "From Teaching to Learning – A New Paradigm for Undergraduate Education." *Change: The Magazine of Higher Learning* 27, no. 6 (1995): 12–26.

Beach, Leslie R. "Self-Directed Student Groups and College Learning." *Higher Education* 3, no. 2 (1974): 187–200. doi:10.1007/BF00143791.

Bean, John C., and Maryellen Weimer. *Engaging Ideas: The Professor's Guide to Integrating Writing, Critical Thinking, and Active Learning in the Classroom*. 2nd ed. San Francisco: Jossey-Bass, 2011.

Bligh, Donald A. *What's the Use of Lectures?* Exeter, UK: Intellect, 1998.

Bloom, Benjamin Samuel. *Taxonomy of Educational Objectives: The Classification of Educational Goals*. New York: Longmans, Green, 1956.

Blum, Susan Debra. *My Word! Plagiarism and College Culture*. Ithaca, NY: Cornell University Press, 2010.

Bowen, José Antonio. *Teaching Naked: How Moving Technology out of Your College Classroom Will Improve Student Learning*. San Francisco: Jossey-Bass, 2012.

Boyer, Ernest L. *Scholarship Reconsidered: Priorities of the Professoriate*. San Francisco: Jossey-Bass, 1997.

Brackett, Virginia. "Inspiring Student Self-Motivation." *InSight: A Collection of Faculty Scholarship* 2 (2007): 26–31.

Bunge, Nancy. "Why I No Longer Teach Online." *Chronicle of Higher Education*," 6 November 2011. Available online at http://www.chronicle.com/article/Why-I-No-Longer-Teach-Online/129615/, accessed 15 December 2016.

Chickering, A.W., and Z.F. Gamson. "Seven Principles for Good Practice in Undergraduate Education." *AAHE Bulletin* 39, no. 7 (1987): 3–7.

Christensen, G., A. Steinmetz, B. Alcorn, A. Bennett, D. Woods, and E.J. Emanuel. "The MOOC Phenomenon: Who Takes Massive Open Online Courses and Why?" SSRN Scholarly Paper. Rochester, NY: Social Science Research Network, November 2013. Available online at http://papers.ssrn.com/abstract=2350964.

Clark, Chris. "Seven (+?) Resources for Better PowerPoint." *NspireD2: Learning Technology in Higher Ed*. 1 February 2011. Available online at https://ltlatnd. wordpress.com/2011/02/01/seven-resources-for-better-powerpoint/.

Davis, Barbara Gross. *Tools for Teaching*. San Francisco: Jossey-Bass, 2001.

Eble, Kenneth Eugene. *The Craft of Teaching: [A Guide to Mastering the Professor's Art]*. San Francisco: Jossey-Bass, 1976.

Eliot, T.S. "Tradition and the Individual Talent." *Poetry Foundation*, 13 October 2009. Available online at http://www.poetryfoundation.org/learning/essay/237868?page=1, accessed 13 December 2013.

Ellul, Jacques. *The Technological Society*. Translated by John Wilkinson. New York: Vintage Books, 1964.

Fink, L. Dee. *Creating Significant Learning Experiences: An Integrated Approach to Designing College Courses*. 2nd ed. San Francisco: Jossey-Bass, 2013.

Finkel, Donald L. *Teaching with Your Mouth Shut*. Portsmouth, NH: Boynton/Cook, 2000.

Fish, Stanley Eugene. "The two cultures of educational reform." *New York Times*, 26 August 2013. Available online at http://opinionator.blogs.nytimes.com/2013/08/26/the-two-cultures-of-educational-reform/?_r=0, accessed 15 December 2016.

Freire, Paulo. *Pedagogy of the Oppressed*. 20th anniversary ed. New York: Continuum, 1993.

Grasha, Anthony. *Teaching with Style: A Practical Guide to Enhancing Learning by Understanding Teaching and Learning Styles*. San Bernardino, CA: Alliance, 2002.

Grove, Jack. "The Best Student Excuses." *Inside Higher Ed*, 30 August 2012. Available online at http://www.insidehighered.com/news/2012/08/30/british-lecturer-compiles-best-student-excuses.

Hacker, Andrew, and Claudia Dreifus. "Who's minding the schools?" *New York Times*, 8 June 2013. Available online at http://www.nytimes.com/2013/06/09/opinion/sunday/the-common-core-whos-minding-the-schools.html.

Hardy, G.H. *A Mathematician's Apology*. 1940. Reprint, Cambridge: Cambridge University, 1969.

Heidegger, Martin. *What Is Called Thinking?* Religious Perspectives 21. New York: Harper & Row, 1968.

Helene, A.F., and G.F. Xavier. "Working Memory and Acquisition of Implicit Knowledge by Imagery Training, without Actual Task Performance." *Neuroscience* 139, no. 1 (2006): 401–13.

Hembrooke, Helene, and Geri Gay. "The Laptop and the Lecture: The Effects of Multitasking in Learning Environments." *Journal of Computing in Higher Education* 15, no. 1 (2003): 46–64. http://dx.doi.org/10.1007/BF02940852.

Hoeft, Mary. "Why University Students Don't Read: What Professors Can Do to Increase Compliance." *International Journal for the Scholarship of Teaching and Learning* 6, no. 2 (2012). Available online at http://digitalcommons.georgiasouthern.edu/ij-sotl/vol6/iss2/12/, accessed 8 December 2016.

Holt, Jim. "He Conceived the Mathematics of Roughness." *New York Review of Books*, 23 May 2013.

hooks, bell. *Teaching to Transgress: Education as the Practice of Freedom*. New York: Routledge, 1994.

Lahey, Jessica. "'I Cheated All Throughout High School.'" *Atlantic*, 24 December 2013. Available online at http://www.theatlantic.com/education/archive/2013/12/i-cheated-all-throughout-high-school/282566/.

Lang, James M. *Cheating Lessons: Learning from Academic Dishonesty*. Cambridge, MA: Harvard University Press, 2013.

Lasswell, Harold D. *Psychopathology and Politics*. 1930. Phoenix ed. Chicago: University of Chicago Press, 1977.

Lindsay, Peter."Abstract Teaching for a Concrete World: A Lesson from Plato." *PS: Political Science & Politics* 44, no. 3 (2011): 605–10. doi:10.1017/S1049096511000692.

– "Attending to Attendance." *Chronicle of Higher Education*, 4 February 2015. Available online at http://www.chronicle.com/blogs/conversation/2015/02/04/attending-to-attendance/, accessed 14 December 14.

– "Looking Back (and Forward) on Rousseau's *Emile*." *Journal of Political Science Education* 12, no. 4 (2016): 487–97.

Lowman, Joseph. "Professors as Performers and Motivators." *College Teaching* 42, no. 4 (1994): 137–41.

Marx, Karl. *Economic and Philosophic Manuscripts of 1844*. New York: International Publishers, 1964.

Mayer, Richard E., and Roxana Moreno. "Nine Ways to Reduce Cognitive Load in Multimedia Learning." *Educational Psychologist* 38, no. 1 (2003): 43–52.

Mazard, A., L. Laou, M. Joliot, and E. Mellet. "Neural Impact of the Semantic Content of Visual Mental Images and Visual Percepts." *Cognitive Brain Research* 24, no. 3 (2005): 423–35. doi:10.1016/j.cogbrainres.2005.02.018.

McKeachie, Wilbert James, and Marilla D Svinicki. *McKeachie's Teaching Tips: Strategies, Research, and Theory for College and University Teachers.* 13th ed. Belmont, CA: Wadsworth, Cengage Learning, 2011.

Mcneill, David. "Japanese Fraud Case Highlights Weaknesses in Scientific Publishing." *Chronicle of Higher Education,* 8 October 2012. Available online at http://www. chronicle.com/article/The-Great-Pretender/134876/?cid=at&utm_source=at&utm_ medium=en.

Means, Barbara, Yukie Toyama, Robert Murphy, Marianne Bakai, and Karla Jones. "Evaluation of Evidence-Based Practices in Online Learning: A Meta-Analysis and Review of Online Learning Studies." Washington, DC: Department of Education, Office of Planning, Evaluation, and Policy Development, Policy and Program Studies Service, September 2010. Available online at http://www2.ed.gov/rschstat/ eval/tech/evidence-based-practices/finalreport.pdf.

Montaigne, Michel de. *The Essays: A Selection.* New York: Penguin, 1993.

Mueller, Pam A., and Daniel M. Oppenheimer. "The Pen Is Mightier Than the Keyboard: Advantages of Longhand Over Laptop Note Taking." *Psychological Science,* 23 April 2014. Available online at https://sites.udel.edu/victorp/ files/2010/11/Psychological-Science-2014-Mueller-0956797614524581-1u0h0yu.pdf.

Murdock, Tamera B., and Eric M. Anderman. "Motivational Perspectives on Student Cheating: Toward an Integrated Model of Academic Dishonesty." *Educational Psychologist* 41, no. 3 (2006): 129–45. doi:10.1207/s15326985ep4103_1.

Myers, Isabel Briggs. *Introduction to Type: A Guide to Understanding Your Results on the Myers-Briggs Type Indicator.* 6th ed. Palo Alto, CA: Consulting Psychologists Press, 1998.

Nilson, Linda B. *Teaching at Its Best: A Research-Based Resource for College Instructors.* 3rd ed. San Francisco: Jossey-Bass, 2010.

Pajares, Frank. "Toward a Positive Psychology of Academic Motivation." *Journal of Educational Research* 95, no. 1 (2001): 27–35.

Palmer, Parker J. *The Courage to Teach: Exploring the Inner Landscape of a Teacher's Life.* San Francisco: Jossey-Bass, 1998.

Pashler, Harold, Mark McDaniel, Doug Rohrer, and Robert Bjork. "Learning Styles: Concepts and Evidence." *Psychological Science in the Public Interest* 9, no. 3 (2008): 105–19. doi:10.1111/j.1539-6053.2009.01038.x.

Patrick, Brian C., Jennifer Hisley, Toni Kempler, and Goucher College. "'What's Everybody So Excited About?': The Effects of Teacher Enthusiasm on Student Intrinsic Motivation and Vitality." *Journal of Experimental Education* 68, no. 3 (2000): 217–36.

Piazza, Jared, Jesse M. Bering, and Gordon Ingram. "'Princess Alice Is Watching You': Children's Belief in an Invisible Person Inhibits Cheating." *Journal of Experimental Child Psychology* 109, no. 3 (2011): 311–20. doi:10.1016/j.jecp.2011.02.003.

Radford, Alexandria Walton. "Learning at a Distance: Undergraduate Enrollment in Distance Education Courses and Degree Programs." Statistics in Brief NCES 2012-

154. Washington, DC: Department of Education, October 2011. Available online at http://nces.ed.gov/pubs2012/2012154.pdf.

Ravitch, Diane. "Why I Cannot Support the Common Core Standards." *Diane Ravitch's Blog*, 26 February 2013. Available online at https://dianeravitch.net/2013/02/26/ why-i-cannot-support-the-common-core-standards/.

Reinsmith, William A. *Archetypal Forms in Teaching: A Continuum*. Contributions to the Study of Education 56. New York: Greenwood Press, 1992.

Richtel, Matt. "Technology in schools faces questions on value." *New York Times*, 3 September 2011. Available online at http://www.nytimes.com/2011/09/04/ technology/technology-in-schools-faces-questions-on-value.html.

Roberts, J. M. *History of the World*. New York: Oxford University Press, 1993.

Rodgers, Carol R., and Katherine H. Scott. "The Personal Self and Professional Identity in Learning to Teach." In *Handbook of Research on Teacher Education: Enduring Questions in Changing Contexts*, edited by Marilyn Cochran-Smith, Sharon Feiman-Nenser, D. John McIntyre, and Kelly E. Demers, 732–55. New York: Routledge, 2008.

Roig, Miguel. "Plagiarism and Paraphrasing Criteria of College and University Professors." *Ethics & Behavior* 11, no. 3 (2001): 307–23.

Rousseau, Jean-Jacques. *Emile: Or, On Education*. Edited and translated by Allen Bloom. New York: Basic Books, 1979.

Ryan, Richard M., and Edward L. Deci. "Intrinsic and Extrinsic Motivations: Classic Definitions and New Directions." *Contemporary Educational Psychology* 25, no. 1 (2000): 54–67. doi:10.1006/ceps.1999.1020.

Sabbagh, Karl. *The Riemann Hypothesis: The Greatest Unsolved Problem in Mathematics*. Reprint ed. New York: Farrar, Straus and Giroux, 2004.

Sacks, Oliver. "Speak, Memory." *New York Review of Books*, 21 February 2013. Available online at https://www.nybooks.com/articles/2013/02/21/speak-memory/, accessed 13 December 2016.

Sana, Faria, Tina Weston, and Nicholas J. Cepeda. "Laptop Multitasking Hinders Classroom Learning for Both Users and Nearby Peers." *Computers & Education* 62 (March 2013): 24–31. doi:10.1016/j.compedu.2012.10.003.

Scruton, Roger. "The Idea of a University." *American Spectator*, 17 September 2010. Available online at http://spectator.org/articles/38984/idea-university.

Searle, John R. "Can Information Theory Explain Consciousness?" *New York Review of Books*, 10 January 2013. Available online at http://www.nybooks.com/articles/2013/01/10/ can-information-theory-explain-consciousness/, accessed 15 December 2016.

– "The Mystery of Consciousness Continues." *New York Review of Books*, 9 June 2011. Available online at http://www.nybooks.com/articles/2011/06/09/mystery-consciousness-continues/, accessed 15 December 2016.

Shea, Christopher. "When One Biographer 'Borrows' from Another, the Dispute Gets Philosophical." *Chronicle of Higher Education*, 9 July 2012. Available online at http:// www.chronicle.com/article/When-One-Biographer-Borrows/132705/.

Shell, Duane F., David W. Brooks, Guy Trainin, Kathleen M. Wilson, Douglas F. Kauffman, and Lynne M. Herr. *The Unified Learning Model: How Motivational, Cognitive, and Neurobiological Sciences Inform Best Teaching Practices*. Dordrecht, Netherlands: Springer, 2010.

Simons, Tad. "Does PowerPoint Make You Stupid?" *Presentations.com*, March 2004. Available online at http://www.ltrr.arizona.edu/kkh/dendro/PDFs.Tufte/Does%20 PowerPoint%20Make%20you%20Stupid.pdf.

Smith, Adam. *The Theory of Moral Sentiments*. Glasgow Edition of the Works and Correspondence of Adam Smith, vol. 1. Oxford: Clarendon Press, 1979.

Sorcinelli, Mary Dean. "Promoting Civility in Large Classes." In *Engaging Large Classes: Strategies and Techniques for College Faculty*, edited by Christine A. Stanley and M. Erin Porter, 44–57. Boston: Anker, 2002.

Sousa, David A. *How the Brain Learns: A Classroom Teacher's Guide*. Thousand Oaks, CA: Corwin Press, 2001.

Talbert, Robert. "The Trouble with Khan Academy – Casting Out Nines." *Chronicle of Higher Education*, 3 July 2012. Available online at http://www.chronicle.com/ blognetwork/castingoutnines/2012/07/03/the-trouble-with-khan-academy/, accessed 15 December 2016.

Thompson, William L., Scott D. Slotnick, Marie S. Burrage, and Stephen M. Kosslyn. "Two Forms of Spatial Imagery: Neuroimaging Evidence." *Psychological Science)* 20, no. 10 (2009): 1245–53. doi:10.1111/j.1467-9280.2009.02440.x.

Tokuhama-Espinosa, Tracey. *Mind, Brain, and Education Science: A Comprehensive Guide to the New Brain-Based Teaching*. New York: W.W. Norton, 2011.

Tufte, Edward R. *The Cognitive Style of PowerPoint: Pitching Out Corrupts Within*. 2nd ed. Cheshire, CT: Graphics Press, 2006.

Willingham, Daniel T. "How to get your mind to read." *New York Times*, 25 November 2017. Available online at https://www.nytimes.com/2017/11/25/opinion/sunday/how-to-get-your-mind-to-read.html?action=click&pgtype=Homepage&clickSource=story-heading& module=region&region=region&WT.nav=region&_r=2, accessed 2 December 2017.

– *The Reading Mind: A Cognitive Approach to Understanding How the Mind Reads*. San Francisco: Jossey-Bass, 2017.

– *Why Don't Students Like School? A Cognitive Scientist Answers Questions about How the Mind Works and What It Means for the Classroom*. San Francisco: Jossey-Bass, 2009.

Willis, Judy. *Research-based Strategies to Ignite Student Learning: Insights from a Neurologist and Classroom Teacher*. Alexandria, VA: Association for Supervision and Curriculum Development, 2006.

Zull, James E. "Key Aspects of How the Brain Learns." *New Directions for Adult & Continuing Education* 2006, no. 110 (2006): 3–9. doi:10.1002/ace.213.

– "The Art of Changing the Brain." *Educational Leadership* 62, no. 1 (September 2004): 68–72.

Index